CALIFORNIA TEST PREP
Reading Skills Workbook
Daily SBAC ELA Practice
Grade 4

© 2018 by C. Hawas

All rights reserved. No part of this book may be reproduced or transmitted in any form or by any means, electronic, mechanical, photocopying, recording, or otherwise without prior written permission.

ISBN 978-1726109567

TEST MASTER PRESS

www.testmasterpress.com

CONTENTS

Introduction	4
Reading Comprehension Exercises	**5**
Set 1 – Literary Texts	5
Set 2 – Informational Texts	15
Set 3 – Informational Texts	25
Set 4 – Literary and Informational Texts	35
Set 5 – Literary and Informational Texts	45
Set 6 – Paired Literary Texts	55
Set 7 – Paired Informational Texts	63
Set 8 – Literary Texts	69
Set 9 – Informational Texts	79
Set 10 – Informational Texts	89
Set 11 – Literary and Informational Texts	99
Set 12 – Literary and Informational Texts	109
Set 13 – Paired Literary Texts	119
Set 14 – Paired Informational Texts	127
Answer Key	**133**
Set 1 – Literary Texts	134
Set 2 – Informational Texts	136
Set 3 – Informational Texts	138
Set 4 – Literary and Informational Texts	140
Set 5 – Literary and Informational Texts	142
Set 6 – Paired Literary Texts	144
Set 7 – Paired Informational Texts	146
Set 8 – Literary Texts	148
Set 9 – Informational Texts	150
Set 10 – Informational Texts	152
Set 11 – Literary and Informational Texts	154
Set 12 – Literary and Informational Texts	156
Set 13 – Paired Literary Texts	158
Set 14 – Paired Informational Texts	160

INTRODUCTION
For Parents, Teachers, and Tutors

About the Book

This book will develop the reading skills that students are expected to have, while preparing students for the reading sections of the Smarter Balanced (SBAC) assessments. This workbook covers the skills listed in the Common Core State Standards. The focus of the book is on developing reading skills, but complementary writing and language skills are also covered.

Ongoing Reading Comprehension Practice

The aim of this book is to give students ongoing reading comprehension practice without the stress of long passages and question sets. Each set contains four short texts with questions, or two texts in paired sets. By completing each set, students will gain experience with a range of passage types, become familiar with common question types, practice understanding and responding to texts, develop confidence, and master Common Core reading skills.

Developing Common Core Reading Skills

The state of California has adopted the Common Core State Standards. These standards describe what students are expected to know. The reading standards are divided into two areas: Reading Standards for Literature and Reading Standards for Informational Text. This book includes sets that focus only on literature, only on informational texts, and mixed sets that cover both. The workbook also includes sets with paired passages, where students synthesize and integrate information from two texts.

Introducing Core Skills

Each passage in this book includes a Core Skills Practice exercise that focuses on one key reading, writing, or language skill. These exercises will introduce students to the key skills and help students transition to the more challenging Common Core standards.

Preparing for the Smarter Balanced (SBAC) Assessments

In the 2014-2015 school year, the state of California introduced new assessments. These are the Smarter Balanced, or the SBAC, assessments. The English Language Arts/Literacy assessments cover reading, writing, speaking/listening, and research. This book will prepare students for the reading sections. The reading skills developed are those that will be assessed, so the strong skill development gained will help students perform well. The book provides experience understanding, analyzing, and responding to passages, as well as practice answering selected-response, constructed-response, and technology-enhanced questions.

Reading Comprehension

Set 1

Literary Texts

Instructions

Read each passage. Complete the exercise under each passage.

Then complete the questions following each passage. For each multiple-choice question, fill in the circle for the correct answer. For other types of questions, follow the instructions given. Some of the questions require a written answer. Write your answer on the lines provided.

The Acorn

A man, proud of his wit and his reason,
sat under an oak in a hot summer season.
On the oak grew an acorn or two, it is said:
on the ground grew a pumpkin as big as his head.

    Said the man to himself, "This oak is so very strong,
    why does it hold acorns that are scarce an inch long?
    Yet this poor feeble plant on the ground,
    has to hold up the pumpkins that weigh many pounds?"

But just as he decided nature had made a mistake,
an acorn from the tree did break.
It fell on his head, but did not cause any pain.
And the man decided to never ever question nature again.

CORE SKILLS PRACTICE

How does the acorn falling on the man's head change how he feels about where acorns and pumpkins should grow? Explain your answer.

_____

_____

_____

_____

_____

_____

1   What is the main mistake the man in the poem makes?
    Ⓐ   Believing that acorns are smaller than pumpkins
    Ⓑ   Thinking that he knows better than nature
    Ⓒ   Deciding to sit under an oak tree in summer
    Ⓓ   Talking to himself instead of to other people

2   In the line below, what does the word <u>feeble</u> mean?

    Yet this poor feeble plant on the ground,

    Ⓐ   Cheap
    Ⓑ   Old
    Ⓒ   Lonely
    Ⓓ   Weak

3   Which detail shown in the photographs is most relevant to the events of the poem?
    Ⓐ   Acorns often grow in bunches.
    Ⓑ   Acorns are a type of nut.
    Ⓒ   Pumpkins are much larger than acorns.
    Ⓓ   Pumpkins lie amongst the leaves of the plant.

4   What can be inferred about why the man decides to "never ever question nature again"?
    Ⓐ   He realizes that things are just as they should be.
    Ⓑ   He understands there is nothing he can do about how things are.
    Ⓒ   He sees that he should be grateful for having food and shade.
    Ⓓ   He believes that nature has punished him for questioning things.

Tom's Time Machine

Tom had spent almost a decade designing and building his time machine. He had spent countless hours in his laboratory. After he developed it, he had done many experiments sending small objects through time. And now, after all his hard work, it was finally time to test it for himself. He entered the time machine, and began to type into the computer.

Tom had always wanted to go back to the dinosaur age. He set the time to 80 million years ago. As the machine went dark and began to shake, he knew he was on his way deep into the unknown. He was scared, but thrilled with the idea that he might see a real dinosaur. He just hoped that the first one he saw was a friendly one.

CORE SKILLS PRACTICE

Write a paragraph to add to the end of the story. In your paragraph, describe what happens when Tom sees his first dinosaur.

_____

_____

_____

_____

_____

_____

_____

1 What does the illustration represent?
   Ⓐ   How long it took Tom to create the time machine
   Ⓑ   Where Tom plans to travel to in the time machine
   Ⓒ   What the time machine looks like
   Ⓓ   How the time machine works

2 What type of passage is "Tom's Time Machine"?
   Ⓐ   Science fiction
   Ⓑ   Historical fiction
   Ⓒ   Autobiography
   Ⓓ   Tall tale

3 Which word would Tom most likely use to describe his day?
   Ⓐ   Frightening
   Ⓑ   Confusing
   Ⓒ   Exciting
   Ⓓ   Ordinary

4 The passage says that Tom had spent countless hours in his laboratory. The word countless means –
   Ⓐ   boring
   Ⓑ   very many
   Ⓒ   sad and lonely
   Ⓓ   worthwhile

Making Mistakes

Kelly was trying to do her homework. She had ten division problems, and she couldn't get the first one right. Each time she tried, it was still wrong. The more mistakes she made, the more she rushed, and that led to even more mistakes. She tore another page from her notebook, scrunched it into a ball, and sighed. She didn't know if she wanted to scream or cry.

"It's alright Kelly," her father said. "Everybody makes mistakes. Just stop for a minute, sit back, and take a few deep breaths. You will get it, but you need to clear your mind first."

Her father's words helped to calm Kelly. She leaned back, took a deep breath, and stared out the window. She let go of the pencil she was clutching so tightly and wiggled her fingers. She reminded herself that she could do it, and her anger started to slip away. After a few minutes, she felt better and ready to try again.

She picked her pencil back up, leaned forward, and started the question again. This time, she completed each step slowly. Finally, she arrived at the right answer. She felt good and moved on to the next question with confidence. Before she knew it, she had all her questions completed without a single mistake.

CORE SKILLS PRACTICE

How are Kelly's feelings different in the last paragraph than in the first paragraph? How does this help explain why she gets better results?

_____

_____

_____

_____

_____

1 Read this sentence from the passage.

> **She tore another page from her notebook, scrunched it into a ball, and sighed.**

These actions are described to show that Kelly feels —

- Ⓐ embarrassed
- Ⓑ amused
- Ⓒ tired
- Ⓓ upset

2 Which phrase in the third paragraph creates an image that suggests that Kelly is angry?

- Ⓐ *leaned back*
- Ⓑ *stared out the window*
- Ⓒ *pencil she was clutching so tightly*
- Ⓓ *reminded herself that she could do it*

3 Which word best describes Kelly's father?

- Ⓐ Cranky
- Ⓑ Helpful
- Ⓒ Fun
- Ⓓ Lazy

4 What is the main lesson that is learned in the passage?

- Ⓐ It is important to remain calm.
- Ⓑ Math can sometimes be hard.
- Ⓒ Parents should help their children.
- Ⓓ It is easy to get angry at yourself.

In the End

Michael heard the starting pistol and began to run as fast as he could. As he pulled ahead of Stephen, he felt confident that he would win the race. Michael kept running as fast as he could. He started to get a nice lead. Stephen ran at a steady pace, taking care not to wear himself out.

As they both reached the final straight, Michael began to tire. He had been running so hard that he had no energy left. He began to slow. Stephen maintained his own pace and overtook Michael with his final stride. The race and the gold medal were won by Stephen. Michael walked over and patted Stephen on the back to congratulate him on the win. He was disappointed in himself, but he knew that Stephen had run a better race.

CORE SKILLS PRACTICE

Sometimes you will be asked to compare or contrast two characters. This means that you decide what is similar about the two characters or what is different about the two characters. Contrast Michael and Stephen by answering the question below.

How is Michael's approach to the race different from Stephen's?

_____

_____

_____

_____

_____

1 Read this sentence from the passage.

> **Stephen maintained his own pace and overtook Michael with his final stride.**

As it is used in the sentence, what does <u>maintained</u> mean?

- Ⓐ Increased slightly
- Ⓑ Kept steady
- Ⓒ Looked after
- Ⓓ Improved upon

2 Which statement best describes the theme of the passage?

- Ⓐ Slow and steady wins the race.
- Ⓑ It is better to be safe than sorry.
- Ⓒ There is only one winner.
- Ⓓ Life is full of surprises.

3 How is the passage mainly organized?

- Ⓐ A solution to a problem is described.
- Ⓑ Events are described in the order they occurred.
- Ⓒ Facts are given to support an argument.
- Ⓓ An event in the past is compared to an event today.

4 When does the turning point of the passage occur?

- Ⓐ When the race begins
- Ⓑ When Michael pulls ahead of Stephen
- Ⓒ When Stephen overtakes Michael
- Ⓓ When Michael pats Stephen on the back

5 How does Michael most likely feel after the race? Use information from the passage to support your answer.

Reading Comprehension

Set 2

Informational Texts

Instructions

Read each passage. Complete the exercise under each passage.

Then complete the questions following each passage. For each multiple-choice question, fill in the circle for the correct answer. For other types of questions, follow the instructions given. Some of the questions require a written answer. Write your answer on the lines provided.

The Rubik's Cube

The Rubik's Cube is a three-dimensional mechanical puzzle. It was first invented in 1974. It was designed and created by Hungarian sculptor Erno Rubik. It has six faces covered by nine stickers of six different colors. The challenge is to spin and move the cube until all sides are covered by a single color.

Erno Rubik probably had no idea how popular his toy would become. The cube was licensed to be sold by Ideal Toy Corp in 1980. It has since become one of the world's most successful toys. It has sold over 350 million units.

The Rubik's Cube looks like a simple puzzle to solve at first, but it is actually quite difficult. There is a trick to it and it takes some time to master. Once you learn how to solve the puzzle, the fun is just beginning. There are plenty of ways you can keep challenging yourself.

Solving a Rubik's Cube has become almost like a sport. World championships are held where people compete to solve the puzzle in the shortest amount of time. In 2013, Mats Valk set the record at 5.55 seconds. There are also special categories where people compete to solve the puzzle blindfolded, one-handed, underwater, or with their feet!

CORE SKILLS PRACTICE

The author says that once you learn how to solve the puzzle, the fun is just beginning. Explain how the last paragraph supports this statement.

_____

_____

_____

_____

_____

1 Circle the **two** words from the passage that have about the same meaning.

created   sport   invented   successful   sold

simple   puzzle   compete   difficult   spin

2 Which sentence best supports the idea that the Rubik's Cube is popular?
- Ⓐ *The Rubik's Cube is a three-dimensional mechanical puzzle.*
- Ⓑ *It was designed and created by Hungarian sculptor Erno Rubik.*
- Ⓒ *The cube was licensed to be sold by Ideal Toy Corp in 1980.*
- Ⓓ *It has sold over 350 million units.*

3 Determine which sentences below are facts and which sentences give the author's opinion. Write F or O on each line to show your choice.

___ It was designed by Erno Rubik.

___ Erno Rubik had no idea how popular it would become.

___ It was invented in 1974.

___ It has six faces.

___ It is difficult to solve.

___ It has sold over 350 million units.

4 Which sentence tells how to solve a Rubik's Cube?
- Ⓐ *The Rubik's Cube is a three-dimensional mechanical puzzle.*
- Ⓑ *The challenge is to spin and move the cube until all sides are covered by a single color.*
- Ⓒ *Once you learn how to solve the puzzle, the fun is just beginning.*
- Ⓓ *Solving a Rubik's Cube has become almost like a sport.*

Big Ben

Big Ben is one of the United Kingdom's most famous landmarks. It is located in the Palace of Westminster in London. Big Ben is the term given to refer to the great bell of the clock at the north end of the building. Over time, the nickname has been used to refer to the clock and the clock tower too.

Its building was completed in April 1858, and it celebrated its 150th anniversary in 2009. Even though it is over 150 years old, it still looks beautiful. It looks down on the city like it is keeping watch on the people. One unusual feature is that the clock has four faces, which allows the clock to be seen from every angle. It is actually the largest four-faced chiming clock in the world. It is also the third largest freestanding clock in the world.

CORE SKILLS PRACTICE

Locate the information in the passage to answer the questions below.

In what country is Big Ben located?
_____

In what building is Big Ben located?
_____

When was Big Ben built?
_____

What was celebrated in 2009?
_____

1 Which word means the opposite of <u>beautiful</u>?

Even though it is over 150 years old, it still looks beautiful.

- Ⓐ Lovely
- Ⓑ Ugly
- Ⓒ Old
- Ⓓ Modern

2 What is the main purpose of the passage?
- Ⓐ To inform readers about a famous clock
- Ⓑ To persuade readers to visit Big Ben
- Ⓒ To compare Big Ben to other clocks
- Ⓓ To teach readers how to find the clock

3 Which sentence from the passage contains an opinion?
- Ⓐ *It is located in the Palace of Westminster in London.*
- Ⓑ *Its building was completed in April 1858, and it celebrated its 150th anniversary in 2009.*
- Ⓒ *Even though it is over 150 years old, it still looks beautiful.*
- Ⓓ *It is also the third largest freestanding clock in the world.*

4 The author states that the clock "looks down on the city like it is keeping watch on the people." Which literary technique is used in the statement?
- Ⓐ Personification, describing objects as if they have human qualities
- Ⓑ Symbolism, using an object to stand for something else
- Ⓒ Hyperbole, overstating the qualities of something to make a point
- Ⓓ Alliteration, repeating consonant sounds in neighboring words

Sir Isaac Newton

Sir Isaac Newton is one of the most important scientists that has ever lived. He made many important achievements. He studied math and physics. In today's society, he is best known for stating the laws of gravity.

Isaac Newton also developed laws of motion, or laws that explain how things move. It is a little known fact that he also built one of the first telescopes. Newton developed many theories about mathematics and physics that are still used today.

© Andrew Gray, Wikimedia Commons

CORE SKILLS PRACTICE

The author gives brief information about Isaac Newton. Imagine you want to write a more detailed report about Isaac Newton. What else would you want to include in the report? Write a list of questions you could research and answer in your report.

1. _____

2. _____

3. _____

4. _____

5. _____

6. _____

1. Which meaning of the word underlined developed is used in the sentence below?

   Newton developed many theories about mathematics and physics that are still used today.

   Ⓐ Grew older

   Ⓑ Became larger

   Ⓒ Created

   Ⓓ Ripened

2. How is the passage mainly organized?

   Ⓐ A solution to a problem is described.

   Ⓑ Events are described in the order they occurred.

   Ⓒ Facts are given to support an argument.

   Ⓓ An event in the past is compared to an event today.

3. Which of the following was NOT an achievement of Newton's?

   Ⓐ Building a telescope

   Ⓑ Stating the laws of gravity

   Ⓒ Developing laws of motion

   Ⓓ Creating models of atoms

4. Which word best describes how Isaac Newton is presented in the statue shown in the passage?

   Ⓐ Busy

   Ⓑ Wise

   Ⓒ Proud

   Ⓓ Shy

Mount Mauna Kea

It is well known that Mount Everest is the world's highest mountain above sea level. But what about mountains that start beneath the water's surface? If we look at these, then Mount Mauna Kea is the tallest anywhere in the world.

Mount Mauna Kea is an inactive volcano on the island of Hawaii. It is more than 6 miles tall from the seabed to its summit. This makes Mount Mauna Kea almost 1 mile taller than Mount Everest.

Mount Mauna Kea stretches up from the Pacific Ocean. You can see its snow-capped peak about 4,000 meters above sea level. Its base is hidden far below the water.

© Vadim Kurland, Wikimedia Commons

CORE SKILLS PRACTICE

Imagine you want to add a diagram to make it easier to compare Mount Mauna Kea and Mount Everest. Describe what the diagram would look like.

_____

_____

_____

_____

_____

1 In which word does <u>in</u> mean the same as in the word <u>inactive</u>?

- Ⓐ Instant
- Ⓑ Invent
- Ⓒ Instrument
- Ⓓ Incorrect

2 Which sentence from the passage best summarizes the main idea?

- Ⓐ *It is well known that Mount Everest is the world's highest mountain above sea level.*
- Ⓑ *Mount Mauna Kea is an inactive volcano on the island of Hawaii.*
- Ⓒ *It is more than 6 miles tall from the seabed to its summit.*
- Ⓓ *This makes Mount Mauna Kea almost 1 mile taller than Mount Everest.*

3 If the passage were given another title, which title would best fit?

- Ⓐ All About Mount Everest
- Ⓑ The Real World's Tallest Mountain
- Ⓒ How Mountains Form
- Ⓓ The Dangers of Volcanoes

4 What does the photograph and caption show about Mount Mauna Kea?

- Ⓐ It is taller than it appears.
- Ⓑ It is unlikely to ever erupt.
- Ⓒ It is popular with tourists.
- Ⓓ It is increasing in height.

5 Explain how Mount Everest and Mount Mauna Kea are similar. Explain how Mount Everest and Mount Mauna Kea are different. Use information from the passage to support your answer.

Reading Comprehension

Set 3

Informational Texts

Instructions

Read each passage. Complete the exercise under each passage.

Then complete the questions following each passage. For each multiple-choice question, fill in the circle for the correct answer. For other types of questions, follow the instructions given. Some of the questions require a written answer. Write your answer on the lines provided.

Advertisement

CORE SKILLS PRACTICE

Would you choose the product for breakfast? If so, describe what features you like about it. If not, explain why not.

_____

_____

_____

_____

_____

1. What does the word <u>instant</u> tell readers about the oatmeal?
   - Ⓐ It comes in handy single serve packets.
   - Ⓑ It is a healthy choice.
   - Ⓒ It does not take long to prepare.
   - Ⓓ It contains fresh ingredients.

2. Which statement from the advertisement describes the texture of the oatmeal?
   - Ⓐ Quick & Easy
   - Ⓑ Organic Ingredients
   - Ⓒ Premium Quality
   - Ⓓ Smooth and Creamy

3. What does the art of the oatmeal mainly highlight?
   - Ⓐ It is made from ingredients from local farms.
   - Ⓑ It contains a lot of fruit and berries.
   - Ⓒ It can be served hot or cold.
   - Ⓓ It is enjoyable to eat.

4. Which claim does the advertisement make about the product?
   - Ⓐ It is high in calcium.
   - Ⓑ It is high in fiber.
   - Ⓒ It is low in fat.
   - Ⓓ It is low in sugar.

Bacon Sandwich

Bacon sandwiches make a wonderful breakfast or brunch. They are simple to make, but very tasty. You can add your own twist by adding an egg, avocado, or even banana. It's hard to resist a great bacon sandwich!

CORE SKILLS PRACTICE

The passage states that you can "add your own twist" to the bacon sandwich. Explain what this statement means.

_____

_____

_____

_____

1   Which meaning of the word light is used in Step 2 of the instructions?

    Ⓐ   Bright or well-lit

    Ⓑ   Pale in color

    Ⓒ   Weighing little

    Ⓓ   A small amount

2   Which sentence from the passage tells when to eat a bacon sandwich?

    Ⓐ   *Bacon sandwiches make a wonderful breakfast or brunch.*

    Ⓑ   *They are simple to make, but very tasty.*

    Ⓒ   *You can add your own twist by adding an egg, avocado, or even banana.*

    Ⓓ   *It's hard to resist a great bacon sandwich!*

3   If the ingredients for the bacon sandwich were listed in the order they are used, what would the order be from first to last? Use the numbers 1 through 4 to show the order.

    ____ bacon   ____ bread

    ____ cheese   ____ oil

4   Which detail from the passage does the recipe best support?

    Ⓐ   Bacon sandwiches are tasty.

    Ⓑ   Bacon sandwiches are easy to make.

    Ⓒ   Bacon sandwiches are hard to resist.

    Ⓓ   Bacon sandwiches are good for breakfast or brunch.

Monarch Butterflies

Monarch butterflies are fascinating creatures. They are most famous for their annual migration. Beginning in September every year, the butterflies travel thousands of miles. They travel in large groups. It's pretty remarkable to see hundreds of bright orange butterflies flapping by!

Another interesting fact is that they need milkweed plants to survive. This is the only plant that the insect can eat during the caterpillar stage.

In 2009, monarch butterflies even traveled into space. They were taken on board the International Space Station and bred there. These lucky creatures were able to experience flying in zero gravity.

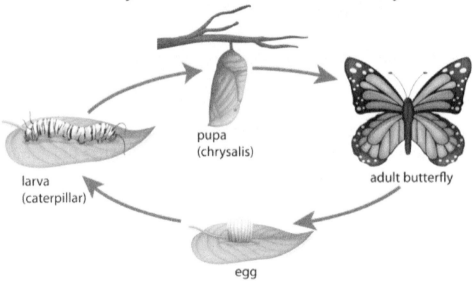

CORE SKILLS PRACTICE

Summarize the information in the passage by listing the **three** reasons the author gives to support the idea that Monarch butterflies are interesting.

1. _____

2. _____

3. _____

1. The passage refers to the "annual migration." Which phrase from the first paragraph helps the reader understand the meaning of <u>annual</u>?
   - Ⓐ "most famous"
   - Ⓑ "every year"
   - Ⓒ "thousands of miles"
   - Ⓓ "large groups"

2. During which stage described in the diagram do the insects need milkweed plants?
   - Ⓐ adult
   - Ⓑ egg
   - Ⓒ larva
   - Ⓓ pupa

3. In the first paragraph, what is the most likely reason the author refers to the butterflies "flapping by"?
   - Ⓐ To suggest that the butterflies move quickly
   - Ⓑ To emphasize that there are large numbers of butterflies
   - Ⓒ To help readers imagine the sight of the butterflies
   - Ⓓ To show that the butterflies can be pests

4. What do the arrows in the diagram indicate about the life cycle?
   - Ⓐ It repeats itself.
   - Ⓑ It happens only once.
   - Ⓒ It takes place quickly.
   - Ⓓ It is fascinating to watch.

Monument Valley

The Monument Valley Navajo Tribal Park is a famous tourist attraction. It is famous because of its beauty and its use in films and ads. It is a well-known icon of the American Southwest. Many people visit Monument Valley Navajo Tribal Park every year to spend time there. Popular activities include hiking, photography, and stargazing.

Monument Valley Navajo Tribal Park is located on the border region of Utah and Arizona. It lies within a Navajo Indian Reservation. The Navajo Nation is one of the largest American Indian tribes. Therefore, the entire park is a very culturally rich region.

Monument Valley Navajo Tribal Park is characterized by large rock formations and red, sandy plains. The rock formations are known as buttes. They are stunning to view.

> **butte** *noun*
> 1. a hill or mountain with steep sides and a flat top

There is a lot of sightseeing to be done in the Monument Valley Navajo Tribal Park. There are tours available to visitors. Many people do self-guided tours, but a guided tour is a good option because the tour guides can provide details about the area. Four-wheel drive tours are also quite popular with visitors.

CORE SKILLS PRACTICE

The passage states that Monument Valley is "a well-known icon of the American Southwest." Explain what this phrase means.

_____

_____

_____

_____

1   What does the art in the passage show?

     Ⓐ   The main reason most people visit the park

     Ⓑ   Why the park is used in films and advertisements

     Ⓒ   An example of an activity people enjoy in the park

     Ⓓ   The best way to experience the beauty of the park

2   Which word best describes the information in the text box?

     Ⓐ   Definition

     Ⓑ   Opinion

     Ⓒ   Source

     Ⓓ   Summary

3   Which of these would be best to add to the passage to represent the information below?

     Monument Valley Navajo Tribal Park is located on the border region of Utah and Arizona. It lies within a Navajo Indian Reservation.

     Ⓐ   Graph

     Ⓑ   Map

     Ⓒ   Timeline

     Ⓓ   Table

4   Based on the passage, why is a guided tour better than a self-guided tour?

     Ⓐ   Visitors are able to learn more.

     Ⓑ   Visitors are safer and do not risk getting lost.

     Ⓒ   Visitors are taken to the most important sites.

     Ⓓ   Visitors are likely to enjoy sharing the experience.

5 Hundreds of thousands of people visit the Monument Valley Navajo Tribal Park each year. What do you think attracts so many people to the park? Use information from the passage to support your answer.

Reading Comprehension

Set 4

Literary and Informational Texts

Instructions

Read each passage. Complete the exercise under each passage.

Then complete the questions following each passage. For each multiple-choice question, fill in the circle for the correct answer. For other types of questions, follow the instructions given. Some of the questions require a written answer. Write your answer on the lines provided.

The Basement Door

Jake had always been scared of the basement. Its heavy wooden door made a long slow creaking cry that sent shivers down his spine. He had only ever peeked through the door from the safety of the hall. The basement was pitch black and seemed to go on forever. Cold air seemed to reach out and circle around him.

Jake's parents had always warned him not to go down there. After hearing this many times, Jake's curious nature finally won him over. He had to know what was down there.

Jake pushed the door open and began to tiptoe down the faded old wooden stairs. As he reached the middle step, he heard a loud bang from deep inside the basement's darkness. He turned sharply and hurried back up the stairs. He never tried to go down into the basement again.

CORE SKILLS PRACTICE

Choose **two** details the author includes to make the basement seem creepy. Explain how each detail makes the basement seem creepy.

1. _____

2. _____

1 Why does Jake leave the basement?

- Ⓐ His parents tell him to.
- Ⓑ The door creaks.
- Ⓒ He hears a loud noise.
- Ⓓ He sees something scary.

2 What is the first paragraph mostly about?

- Ⓐ What the basement door sounds like
- Ⓑ What happens when Jake goes into the basement
- Ⓒ Why Jake decides to go down into the basement
- Ⓓ How Jake feels about the basement

3 The passage states that Jake turned sharply and hurried back up the stairs. What does the word <u>sharply</u> show about Jake?

- Ⓐ He tripped over.
- Ⓑ He turned slowly.
- Ⓒ He turned suddenly.
- Ⓓ He hurt himself.

4 Sensory details can use sight, sound, taste, smell, or touch. Identify the sense used for each detail below. Write the sense on the blank line.

_____ The door makes a long slow creaking cry.

_____ The basement is pitch black.

_____ The cold air seems to reach out and circle Jake.

The Olympics

The Olympics are a global sporting event. They feature both outdoor and indoor sports. They are watched and enjoyed by people all over the world. They are an important event because they bring people from all countries together.

They are held in both a summer and winter format. The Winter Olympics and Summer Olympics are held every 4 years. The first modern Olympics were held in 1896. Many nations compete in each Olympic event. A different country hosts the games each time. The city of London in the United Kingdom was the host in 2012. The 2016 games will be held in Rio de Janeiro in Brazil.

Year	Held
2012	London, United Kingdom
2008	Beijing, China
2004	Athens, Greece
2000	Sydney, Australia
1996	Atlanta, United States
1992	Barcelona, Spain

CORE SKILLS PRACTICE

It can take years of training to win an Olympic medal. People often have to give up a lot to even compete in the Olympics. Do you think winning an Olympic medal is a worthwhile goal? Explain your answer.

_____

_____

_____

_____

1 Which sentence from the passage is an opinion?

- Ⓐ *They are an important event because they bring people from all countries together.*
- Ⓑ *The Winter Olympics and Summer Olympics are held every 4 years.*
- Ⓒ *The first modern Olympics were held in 1896.*
- Ⓓ *The city of London in the United Kingdom was the host in 2012.*

2 Which word means about the same as <u>global</u>?

- Ⓐ Athletic
- Ⓑ Worldwide
- Ⓒ Popular
- Ⓓ Recent

3 Based on your answer to Question 2, which sentence best shows the meaning of <u>global</u>?

- Ⓐ *They feature both outdoor and indoor sports.*
- Ⓑ *They are watched and enjoyed by people all over the world.*
- Ⓒ *They are held in both a summer and winter format.*
- Ⓓ *The first modern Olympics were held in 1896.*

4 According to the table, in which year were the Olympic Games held in America?

- Ⓐ 2008
- Ⓑ 2004
- Ⓒ 2000
- Ⓓ 1996

Air

You may think of oxygen as the main gas in air, but it is actually nitrogen. Nitrogen accounts for 78 percent of the air that we breathe. Surprisingly, only 21 percent of the air is made up of oxygen.

The high amount of nitrogen in the air is the result of volcanic eruptions during the Earth's early history. Less than 1 percent of air is made up of carbon dioxide. Argon is the only other major gas in air. It accounts for less than 1 percent of its makeup.

CORE SKILLS PRACTICE

Many passages include photographs. These support the information in the passage. Describe what the photograph helps the reader understand.

_____

_____

_____

_____

1   How is the first paragraph organized?
    Ⓐ   A problem is described and then a solution is given.
    Ⓑ   Events are described in the order they occurred.
    Ⓒ   A statement is made and then facts are given to support it.
    Ⓓ   A cause is described and then its effect is shown.

2   Place the gases in order from the highest amount in the air to the lowest amount in the air. Write 1, 2, 3, and 4 on the lines to show the order.

    _____ Argon

    _____ Carbon dioxide

    _____ Nitrogen

    _____ Oxygen

3   Which of the following would be best to add to the passage to support the information?
    Ⓐ   A timeline of the major events in the Earth's history
    Ⓑ   A graph showing how much of each gas makes up the atmosphere
    Ⓒ   A photograph showing what the atmosphere looks like
    Ⓓ   A table describing the atmospheres of different planets

4   Which sentence from the passage gives a cause and effect?
    Ⓐ   *You may think of oxygen as the main gas in air, but it is actually nitrogen.*
    Ⓑ   *Nitrogen accounts for 78 percent of the air that we breathe.*
    Ⓒ   *The high amount of nitrogen in the air is the result of volcanic eruptions during the Earth's early history.*
    Ⓓ   *Argon is the only other major gas in air.*

Visiting the Circus

Mickey didn't like clowns. When his family told him that he would be going to the circus, he was excited. He knew there would be lions, camels, and a trapeze artist. Then he remembered that there would also be clowns. He became very nervous.

"Don't worry," said his father. "You'll be fine. Your mother and I will be with you."

Mickey felt a little better and decided to go. He took his seat in the front row of the audience. As the clowns came out onto the stage, Mickey froze. Mickey's father took hold of his hand and squeezed it gently. Mickey thought about running off, even though he wasn't really sure what he was afraid of. But he sat quietly in his seat reminding himself over and over that there was nothing to fear. His hands shook a little, but he managed to stay quite calm. Gradually, his feelings of fear faded away. He started to smile as the clowns pranced around. By the time the performance was over, Mickey was giggling along with everyone else in the audience.

CORE SKILLS PRACTICE

You can tell a lot about characters by what they do. Think about what Mickey does in the story. How can you tell that Mickey is afraid?

_____

_____

_____

_____

_____

1 Read this sentence from the passage.

> **Mickey's father took hold of his hand and squeezed it gently.**

What does the word <u>gently</u> mean in the sentence above?

- Ⓐ Firmly
- Ⓑ Quietly
- Ⓒ Softly
- Ⓓ Kindly

2 What is Mickey's main problem in the passage?

- Ⓐ He is afraid of seeing the clowns.
- Ⓑ He does not want to see the lions.
- Ⓒ He wants to go to the circus with his friends.
- Ⓓ He does not understand that clowns are funny.

3 The author says that "Mickey froze" when the clowns came out onto the stage. Why does the author say this?

- Ⓐ To show that Mickey was surprised
- Ⓑ To emphasize how scared Mickey felt
- Ⓒ To explain why Mickey was afraid
- Ⓓ To suggest that Mickey was acting

4 Who is telling the story?

- Ⓐ Mickey
- Ⓑ Mickey's father
- Ⓒ A clown
- Ⓓ Someone not in the story

5 What details in the passage suggest that Mickey is brave? Use information from the passage to support your answer.

Reading Comprehension

Set 5

Literary and Informational Texts

Instructions

Read each passage. Complete the exercise under each passage.

Then complete the questions following each passage. For each multiple-choice question, fill in the circle for the correct answer. For other types of questions, follow the instructions given. Some of the questions require a written answer. Write your answer on the lines provided.

Beneath the Stars

Brian loved camping. He liked to take his family every summer. They would drive up near the lake and find a peaceful spot far from everything. They would pitch their tents on the first day and spend the night beneath the stars. They would swim and hike and go rafting during the day. Brian would often spend time trying to catch fish to have for dinner. Each day was filled with adventures, but it was the nights that Brian looked forward to most.

Brian and his family would huddle around the fire together. With no television or computers, there was nothing to do but chat. Brian's twin sons would tell him more about their lives than he had heard in weeks at home. Sometimes Brian would tell his family his own stories of camping with his father when he was young. Alice, his younger daughter, was a little scared of the dark. At home, she had a radio she would listen to and a night light next to her bed. Away from home, she needed her father again. As they sat in the moonlight, Brian sang her a lullaby to calm her. She slowly drifted off to sleep and enjoyed the most wonderful dreams.

CORE SKILLS PRACTICE

How does not having television or computers affect the family? How does this help explain why Brian enjoys camping so much?

_____

_____

_____

_____

_____

1 Which phrase in the passage creates an image of calmness?

- Ⓐ *drive up near the lake*
- Ⓑ *swim and hike and go rafting*
- Ⓒ *tell his family his own stories*
- Ⓓ *slowly drifted off to sleep*

2 Which word would Brian most likely use to describe the camping trips?

- Ⓐ Exciting
- Ⓑ Stressful
- Ⓒ Scary
- Ⓓ Relaxing

3 What does Brian enjoy most about the camping trips?

- Ⓐ Finding the perfect camping spot
- Ⓑ Catching fish to cook for dinner
- Ⓒ Spending time with his family
- Ⓓ Having outdoor adventures each day

4 As it is used in the passage, what does the word <u>pitch</u> mean?

- Ⓐ To throw
- Ⓑ To suggest an idea
- Ⓒ To set up
- Ⓓ To sway from side to side

The Dodo

The dodo was a species of flightless bird that became extinct. It lived on the island of Mauritius. It lived in an environment free from ground-based predators. When humans arrived on the island, they brought with them many ground-based animals. These included rats, pigs, and dogs. These animals ate dodo's eggs from their nests. The eggs were easy to get to because the nests were on the ground. Humans also hunted dodos for their meat. Humans also destroyed the dodo's forest habitats. The number of dodos decreased until they became extinct.

The dodo will always be remembered because it led to a common phrase. The slang phrase "as dead as a dodo" is used to describe something that is gone forever or definitely dead.

CORE SKILLS PRACTICE

Imagine you are asked to write a report on the dodo. Write a paragraph explaining why the dodo became extinct. You can use the information in the passage, but be sure to explain why the dodo became extinct in your own words.

_____

_____

_____

_____

_____

_____

1   Why did the author most likely include the second paragraph?
    Ⓐ   To tell an interesting detail about the dodo
    Ⓑ   To explain why dodos became extinct
    Ⓒ   To inform readers about how dodos lived
    Ⓓ   To suggest that the dodo should have been saved

2   Which of the following is NOT a reason that the dodo became extinct?
    Ⓐ   It was hunted for meat.
    Ⓑ   Its habitat was destroyed.
    Ⓒ   Its eggs were eaten by animals.
    Ⓓ   It caught human diseases.

3   How was the dodo different from most birds today?
    Ⓐ   It had wings.
    Ⓑ   It laid eggs.
    Ⓒ   Its nests were on the ground.
    Ⓓ   It had a number of predators.

4   In which sentence does <u>free</u> mean the same as in the third sentence?
    Ⓐ   The dog broke <u>free</u> from his lead and raced away.
    Ⓑ   I am so busy that I have hardly any <u>free</u> time at all.
    Ⓒ   On Mondays, the diner offers <u>free</u> dessert with any meal.
    Ⓓ   I cleaned my room so well that it was <u>free</u> of any sign of mess.

Dearest Donna

One year together, one year of bliss,
You brighten my days with your tender kiss.
I hope that you'll be my sweet valentine,
And say that you will always be mine.

In a few years we may well get married,
On the wings of love we'll be carried.
As we grow old as one and together,
Side by side as partners for ever.

CORE SKILLS PRACTICE

Poets sometimes write poems for a certain audience. This poem has an audience of just one person. Explain who the poem was written for and why the poet wrote the poem.

_____

_____

_____

_____

_____

_____

1 What is the tone of the poem?

- Ⓐ Sad
- Ⓑ Cheerful
- Ⓒ Playful
- Ⓓ Loving

2 What is the rhyme pattern of each stanza of the poem?

- Ⓐ Every line rhymes.
- Ⓑ The second and fourth lines rhyme.
- Ⓒ The first and last lines rhyme.
- Ⓓ There are two sets of rhyming lines.

3 The first line refers to one year of bliss. What does the word <u>bliss</u> mean?

- Ⓐ Being alone
- Ⓑ Being married
- Ⓒ Great happiness
- Ⓓ A feeling of concern

4 What does the second stanza of the poem mainly express?

- Ⓐ The poet's hopes for the future
- Ⓑ The poet's reason for writing the poem
- Ⓒ The poet's main problem
- Ⓓ The poet's worries and fears

Letter to the Editor

Dear Editor,

I am worried that our town park does not look as nice as it once did. It is not as well-cared for and is not cleaned as often. The trash cans are sometimes overflowing, and the grass isn't mowed as much as it should be. There are food wrappers, cans, and even broken glass lying around. I've noticed that there is a lot of graffiti appearing too. It does not look inviting at all. Many people that used to take their kids there or walk their dogs there are now avoiding the park.

I think that something must be done about this! It is no longer a lovely place to spend time. It is not even a safe place to play with all the trash lying around. The people of our town need to demand that something be done. It's our park, it could be lovely, and everyone should be able to use it safely and happily.

Yours with hope,

Evan

CORE SKILLS PRACTICE

What details does Evan give to support the idea that the park is not inviting?

_____

_____

_____

_____

_____

1 The author says that the park is not a safe place to play. What item found in the park best supports this idea?

- Ⓐ Food wrappers
- Ⓑ Cans
- Ⓒ Broken glass
- Ⓓ Graffiti

2 What is the main purpose of the passage?

- Ⓐ To encourage people to visit the park
- Ⓑ To convince people that the park must be cleaned up
- Ⓒ To compare the park today with how the park was before
- Ⓓ To describe the different uses of the park

3 Which word means about the same as <u>demand</u>?

The people of our town need to demand that something be done.

- Ⓐ Offer
- Ⓑ Insist
- Ⓒ Plan
- Ⓓ Agree

4 Which sentence would Evan most likely agree with?

- Ⓐ People should keep using the park even if it is poorly looked after.
- Ⓑ People need to make more effort to spend time outdoors.
- Ⓒ People would probably be happy to help clean up the park.
- Ⓓ People would use the park more if it was looked after.

5 How does Evan show how the poor state of the park is affecting people? Give at least **two** ways that people are affected in your answer.

Reading Comprehension

Set 6

Paired Literary Texts

Instructions

This set contains a pair of passages. Read each passage on its own first. Complete the exercise under each passage. Then complete the questions following each passage.

For each multiple-choice question, fill in the circle for the correct answer. For other types of questions, follow the instructions given. Some of the questions require a written answer. Write your answer on the lines provided.

After reading both passages, you will answer one or more additional questions. You will use information from both passages to answer these questions. Write your answers on the lines provided.

Peace and Not War

Terry was watching football in the living room, when his younger brother Mark walked in and changed the channel. Mark was determined to watch his favorite cartoon. They fought over the remote control. Then they started arguing.

"I hate watching football," Mark yelled. "It goes forever and it's boring."

"I hate cartoons," Terry yelled back. "They're stupid and not even funny."

Their voices got louder and louder. The living room began to sound like a zoo. Their mother came in from the kitchen. Without saying anything, she picked up the remote and turned off the television.

"If you can't watch the television nicely, then you can't watch it at all," she said.

"This is all your fault," Terry yelled. "I was enjoying myself and you ruined it."

Mark didn't like being blamed and began yelling back. The fight over whose fault it was went on and on. Finally, their mother stomped in and pointed to the door.

"If you're going to fight like animals, you can go outside like animals," she said.

Mark and Terry both slunk quietly out of the house.

CORE SKILLS PRACTICE

The author says that the living room began to sound like a zoo. What does the author mean by this? Is this a good way to help readers imagine the scene?

_____

_____

_____

_____

_____

1 How is Mark different from Terry?

- Ⓐ He wants to watch television.
- Ⓑ He dislikes watching football.
- Ⓒ He yells louder.
- Ⓓ He dislikes cartoons.

2 Why did the mother most likely go into the living room?

- Ⓐ Because she had finished cooking
- Ⓑ Because she wanted to watch television
- Ⓒ Because she heard her sons fighting
- Ⓓ Because she wanted her sons to do their homework

3 What is the main lesson that the brothers learn in the passage?

- Ⓐ It is important to be quiet when inside.
- Ⓑ It is better to find a way to agree than to fight.
- Ⓒ Television is not important.
- Ⓓ There are too many programs on television.

4 What does the word <u>nicely</u> mean?

- Ⓐ One who is nice
- Ⓑ In a nice way
- Ⓒ Without being nice
- Ⓓ More nice

The Waggiest Tail

Melanie and Becky both had puppies. They took them to the park together twice a week. The puppies would play and chase each other. Melanie and Becky would sit back and watch, often laughing at how much fun their dogs were having.

"My dog has a waggier tail than yours," said Melanie, as they walked home one day.

"Oh, no she doesn't," said Becky. "My dog's tail wags way more. Look at it go!"

Melanie and Becky argued about it the rest of the way home. When they got home, they asked Melanie's mother which dog had the waggiest tail. Melanie's mother watched the dogs closely for a few minutes.

"They both have very waggy tails," she said. "So they are both happy dogs. Isn't that the most important thing?"

Melanie and Becky looked at their dogs. Their tails were still wagging. They smiled at each other and agreed that it didn't matter whose dog had the waggiest tail. It was clear that they were both very happy dogs.

CORE SKILLS PRACTICE

The words "waggier" and "waggiest" are not really words, but the author uses them anyway. Why do you think the author uses these words?

_____

_____

_____

_____

5 Which statement best explains how you can tell that the passage is realistic fiction?

- Ⓐ The events take place outdoors.
- Ⓑ The events described could really happen.
- Ⓒ The passage has a girl as the main character.
- Ⓓ The passage contains facts and opinions.

6 Which statement best describes what the passage is about?

- Ⓐ Two girls with unhappy dogs
- Ⓑ Two girls that fight about everything
- Ⓒ Two girls that argue about something silly
- Ⓓ Two girls that like playing in the park

7 Based on the passage, what does a wagging tail show about a dog?

- Ⓐ It is fit.
- Ⓑ It is hungry.
- Ⓒ It is happy.
- Ⓓ It is thirsty.

8 Which word best describes the mother in the passage?

- Ⓐ Wise
- Ⓑ Patient
- Ⓒ Stern
- Ⓓ Curious

9 What does the author want the reader to learn from Melanie and Becky? Use information from the passage to support your answer.

Directions: Use both passages to answer the following questions.

10   Compare the mother in "Peace and Not War" with the mother in "The Waggiest Tail." Which mother is the most upset with the fighting?

_____
_____
_____
_____
_____
_____

11   The problem in both passages is that two characters are fighting. Is the problem solved in each passage? Explain your answer.

_____
_____
_____
_____
_____
_____

12 What lesson about arguing with your friends or relatives did you learn from the passages? Explain how you could use the lesson in your own life. Use information from both passages to support your answer.

Reading Comprehension

Set 7

Paired Informational Texts

Instructions

This set contains a pair of passages. Read each passage on its own first. Complete the exercise under each passage. Then complete the questions following each passage.

For each multiple-choice question, fill in the circle for the correct answer. For other types of questions, follow the instructions given. Some of the questions require a written answer. Write your answer on the lines provided.

After reading both passages, you will answer one or more additional questions. You will use information from both passages to answer these questions. Write your answers on the lines provided.

Pompeii

Ancient Pompeii is a partially buried Roman city in southern Italy. It was partly destroyed and completely buried after the eruption of Mount Vesuvius in 79AD. The eruption was one of the largest of all time. Lava flowed out of the volcano rapidly. In fact, around 1.5 million tons of lava flowed out per second. Ash, stones, and fumes were thrown high into the air. They formed a cloud of material that reached heights of over 20 miles. The town of Pompeii was right in the path of the volcano. Material rained down from the sky to cover it, and lava later flowed over it. The remains of Pompeii lay hidden under ash and rock for 1,500 years.

Despite being buried by over 4 meters of ash, the city was rediscovered in 1599. It has since been excavated and preserved. It is now one of the most popular tourist attractions in Italy. Over two million people visit Pompeii every year to see the remains of the buildings from almost two thousand years ago.

Notes
Excavated – to remove soil or earth by digging
Preserved – to keep from spoiling

CORE SKILLS PRACTICE

The author includes facts to show how powerful the eruption of Mount Vesuvius was. List **two** facts included for this purpose.

1. _____

_____

2. _____

_____

1 What does the word rediscovered mean?

> **Despite being buried by over 4 meters of ash, the city was rediscovered in 1599.**

- Ⓐ Discovered before
- Ⓑ Discovered again
- Ⓒ Not discovered
- Ⓓ Less discovered

2 What is the main purpose of the notes at the end of the passage?
- Ⓐ To list important details about Pompeii
- Ⓑ To describe how Ancient Pompeii was found
- Ⓒ To give the meaning of difficult words
- Ⓓ To indicate the sources the author used

3 The passage was probably written mainly to –
- Ⓐ teach people about an ancient site
- Ⓑ persuade readers to visit Italy
- Ⓒ tell an entertaining story
- Ⓓ warn readers about volcanoes

4 Which sentence shows that the author is amazed that Pompeii survived?
- Ⓐ *Ancient Pompeii is a partially buried Roman city in southern Italy.*
- Ⓑ *They formed a cloud of material that reached heights of over 20 miles.*
- Ⓒ *Despite being buried by over 4 meters of ash, the city was rediscovered in 1599.*
- Ⓓ *It is now one of the most popular tourist attractions in Italy.*

Volcanoes

Hot magma and gases build up inside our Earth's crust. Every now and then, it bursts out from under the Earth's surface. The result is a volcano.

Think of a volcano as the Earth relieving internal pressure. When a volcano blows, rocks and ash are thrown out high into the atmosphere. Hot magma flows out of a volcano like a river. Magma above the Earth's surface is called lava. If you touched lava with a steel rod, it would melt in seconds. As it moves across the land, it even melts the rock underneath it.

This image shows the eruption of Mount Pinatubo in the Philippines in 1991. It was the second largest eruption of the twentieth century.

CORE SKILLS PRACTICE

Sometimes you will be asked to compare or contrast two things. This means that you decide what is similar about the two things or what is different about the two things. Contrast magma and lava by answering the question below.

How is lava different from magma?

_____

_____

_____

_____

5 Why does the author include the sentence below?

If you touched lava with a steel rod, it would melt in seconds.

- Ⓐ To show how fast lava moves
- Ⓑ To explain where lava comes from
- Ⓒ To emphasize how hot lava is
- Ⓓ To indicate how explosive volcanoes are

6 Which sentence from the passage contains a simile?

- Ⓐ *Hot magma and gases build up inside our Earth's crust.*
- Ⓑ *Think of a volcano as the Earth relieving internal pressure.*
- Ⓒ *When a volcano blows, rocks and ash are thrown out high into the atmosphere.*
- Ⓓ *Hot magma flows out of a volcano like a river.*

7 Which words from the passage indicate the force of a volcano?

- Ⓐ *magma, lava*
- Ⓑ *bursts, blows*
- Ⓒ *rocks, ash*
- Ⓓ *flows, melt*

8 What does the photograph of the eruption mainly show?

- Ⓐ How much magma flows out
- Ⓑ How high rocks and ash reach
- Ⓒ How hot the lava produced is
- Ⓓ How suddenly eruptions can occur

Directions: Use both passages to answer the following question.

9 Describe how volcanoes are powerful events that can harm areas around them. Use details from both passages to support your answer.

Reading Comprehension

Set 8

Literary Texts

Instructions

Read each passage. Complete the exercise under each passage.

Then complete the questions following each passage. For each multiple-choice question, fill in the circle for the correct answer. For other types of questions, follow the instructions given. Some of the questions require a written answer. Write your answer on the lines provided.

Sarah's Diary

Ever since she had been a little girl, Sarah had always written her thoughts in a diary. Although she felt comfortable talking to her sister and parents, she liked to record the details of her day. Sarah found it comforting and it helped her to relax at the end of a long day. If something had gone wrong that day, Sarah would write about it and how it made her feel. She always felt better at the end. Even if she had felt angry or upset to begin with, those emotions would be gone by the time she had finished.

Sometimes when Sarah was alone, she would flick through her diary and read her past entries. She would look back at days where she was sad and think about just how far she had come. She would read about a day when she was so angry with a friend, and the fight would seem silly now. She would read about a good day and relive great times.

Sarah's mother thought it was a good way to spend an hour each afternoon. Sarah's sister often wondered what Sarah was writing about. But she knew she must not read her sister's diary.

CORE SKILLS PRACTICE

The passage describes how Sarah finds writing in her diary relaxing. Use information from the passage to explain how writing in the diary relaxes Sarah.

_____

_____

_____

_____

_____

1 The passage says that Sarah found writing in her diary comforting. What does the word <u>comforting</u> mean?

- Ⓐ Calming
- Ⓑ Challenging
- Ⓒ Upsetting
- Ⓓ Exciting

2 Based on the passage, which word best describes Sarah?

- Ⓐ Outgoing
- Ⓑ Shy
- Ⓒ Caring
- Ⓓ Thoughtful

3 Which sentence best supports the idea that writing in her diary helps Sarah see things clearly?

- Ⓐ *Although she felt comfortable talking to her sister and parents, she liked to record the details of her day.*
- Ⓑ *If something had gone wrong that day, Sarah would write about it and how it made her feel.*
- Ⓒ *She would read about a day when she was so angry with a friend, and the fight would seem silly now.*
- Ⓓ *She would read about a good day and relive great times.*

4 In which sentence does <u>record</u> mean the same as in the passage?

- Ⓐ Jamie broke the <u>record</u> for the most points scored in a game.
- Ⓑ Fiona listened to the songs on an old <u>record</u> her grandma gave her.
- Ⓒ Our group had to <u>record</u> the results of the science experiment.
- Ⓓ My friend does not have a good <u>record</u> of being on time.

Penny the Princess

Penny was a beautiful princess. She lived in a tall towering castle that almost reached the clouds. What people didn't know was that she had special wishing powers. But Penny often failed to use them because she had everything she had ever wanted. She had no need to wish for food, or pretty things, or happy times. Every day was pleasant for Penny.

One day, a poor man visited her and asked for help. He explained that he had lost his crops and his home in a terrible storm. He spent every day out searching for enough food to feed his family, and his poor wife often had to search for food too. He said he would do anything to be able to provide for his family again. Penny agreed to help him right away. She used her powers to wish that the man's land and home would be returned to new. Penny was shocked by how pleased the man was. He jumped up and down, clapped his hands, and a tear even rolled down his cheek. She had never realized how lucky she was. From that day forward, she decided to use her powers to help as many people as she could.

CORE SKILLS PRACTICE

Many stories involve cause and effect. The cause is the reason for something. The effect is what happens. Answer the question about cause and effect.

What effect does meeting the poor man have on Penny?

_____

_____

_____

_____

_____

_____

1 The second sentence says that Penny "lived in a tall towering castle that almost reached the clouds." Which literary device is used in the sentence?

- Ⓐ Simile, comparing the castle to a cloud
- Ⓑ Personification, describing the castle as if it is a person
- Ⓒ Metaphor, showing that the castle is like a cloud
- Ⓓ Hyperbole, overstating how tall the castle is

2 How does Penny change in the passage?

- Ⓐ She realizes how much she can help others.
- Ⓑ She realizes that she has everything she needs.
- Ⓒ She realizes that she has special wishing powers.
- Ⓓ She realizes that she has used her wishes too often.

3 Which term best describes the passage?

- Ⓐ Historical fiction
- Ⓑ Science fiction
- Ⓒ Autobiography
- Ⓓ Fairy tale

4 Based on your answer to Question 3, select the **two** features of the passage that best show what genre it is.

- ☐ It involves magic.
- ☐ It is set in the past.
- ☐ It has a happy ending.
- ☐ It has a female main character.

The Eagle
By Alfred Lord Tennyson

He clasps the crag with crooked hands;
Close to the sun in lonely lands,
Ring'd with the azure[1] world, he stands.

The wrinkled sea beneath him crawls;
He watches from his mountain walls,
And like a thunderbolt he falls.

© Wikimedia Commons/JJ Harrison

_____
[1] azure - a shade of blue

CORE SKILLS PRACTICE

What do you think the eagle is watching in the poem? Why does he dive down at the end? Explain your answer.

_____
_____
_____
_____
_____
_____
_____

1   How many stanzas does the poem have? Circle the correct answer.

    1   2   3   4   5   6

2   In the line below, what does the word "wrinkled" show?

    The wrinkled sea beneath him crawls;

    Ⓐ   How old the sea is
    Ⓑ   What the sea looks like
    Ⓒ   How cold the sea is
    Ⓓ   What color the sea is

3   Why does the poet compare the eagle to a thunderbolt in the last line?
    Ⓐ   To highlight that the eagle is part of nature
    Ⓑ   To suggest that the eagle should be feared
    Ⓒ   To show that the eagle moves silently
    Ⓓ   To emphasize the eagle's speed

4   Hyperbole is overstating something to make a point. The poet uses hyperbole by describing the eagle as "close to the sun." What is the poet trying to show about the eagle?
    Ⓐ   How beautiful he looks
    Ⓑ   How patient he is
    Ⓒ   How high up he is
    Ⓓ   How warm he is

Crying Wolf

Jack sometimes liked to pretend that he was sick so he could have the day off school. He knew his parents were busy in the morning and wouldn't have time to find out if he was really sick. He would begin his act during breakfast by claiming he wasn't hungry. He would sit there looking tired until his mother asked him if everything was all right. He would claim he had a headache, or a stomachache, or just didn't feel right. His mother would send him to bed and promise to drop in to visit him during the day. Jack would hide his smile as he promised he just needed some rest.

After his parents had left for work, Jack would sneak back downstairs and eat some food. Then he would spend the day in bed playing video games, watching movies, and reading. Unfortunately for Jack, he tried the trick too many times and his parents figured out what he was doing.

One day Jack really was feeling unwell, and so he told his parents the moment he woke up. His mother and father didn't pay much attention. They just made him eat some breakfast and sent him off to school. Jack felt ill all day, but he knew he had nobody to blame but himself. He never pretended to be ill again.

CORE SKILLS PRACTICE

In what way is Jack's plan for getting out of school selfish? Explain your answer.

_____

_____

_____

_____

_____

1 What will Jack most likely do the next time he does not want to go to school?

- Ⓐ Tell his parents that he is ill
- Ⓑ Accept that he has to go to school
- Ⓒ Make up a better excuse for not going
- Ⓓ Tell his teacher that he feels unwell

2 Why do Jack's parents send him to school when he says that he is ill?

- Ⓐ They think that school is too important.
- Ⓑ They want to teach him a lesson.
- Ⓒ They do not believe that he is ill.
- Ⓓ They believe that he will get getter soon.

3 What lesson does Jack learn in the passage?

- Ⓐ Look after yourself.
- Ⓑ Listen to your parents.
- Ⓒ Always be truthful.
- Ⓓ Small lies are not harmful.

4 In which word does <u>un</u> mean the same as in <u>unwell</u>?

- Ⓐ Unclear
- Ⓑ Understand
- Ⓒ Uniform
- Ⓓ Unite

5 What is the main lesson that readers can learn from the passage? Use information from the passage to support your answer.

Reading Comprehension

Set 9

Informational Texts

Instructions

Read each passage. Complete the exercise under each passage.

Then complete the questions following each passage. For each multiple-choice question, fill in the circle for the correct answer. For other types of questions, follow the instructions given. Some of the questions require a written answer. Write your answer on the lines provided.

Soccer

Soccer is a ball sport that was invented in England in the 1800s. Each match sees two teams of 11 players compete against each other. The object of the game is to work the ball into one of the two goals positioned at each end of the field. Players can use any part of their bodies, but the ball mustn't touch the arms or hands. A goalkeeper at each end protects the goal, and only this player is allowed to use the hands and arms.

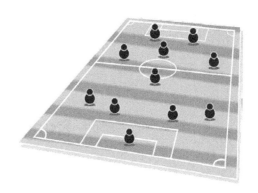

Soccer is not as popular as sports like baseball and basketball in the United States. However, it is a very entertaining sport to watch. Soccer is known for being a low-scoring game. It is common for teams to score only one or two goals in a game and sometimes no goals at all. Some people believe this makes soccer boring to watch, but this is really what makes soccer so exciting. Imagine the thrill of a goal finally being scored after over an hour of play! Fans and players are known for the excitement they show when goals are scored. Soccer may become a favorite sport in the United States one day.

CORE SKILLS PRACTICE

Do you agree that soccer being a low-scoring game would make it exciting? Explain why you do or do not agree.

_____

_____

_____

_____

_____

1   Which meaning of the word <u>object</u> is used in the sentence below?

   The object of the game is to work the ball into one of the two goals positioned at each end of the field.

   Ⓐ   A goal or aim
   Ⓑ   A type of item
   Ⓒ   To argue against
   Ⓓ   To refuse to do something

2   Which sentence from the passage gives the author's personal opinion?
   Ⓐ   *Soccer is a ball sport that was invented in England in the 1800s.*
   Ⓑ   *Players can use any part of their bodies, but the ball mustn't touch the arms or hands.*
   Ⓒ   *It is common for teams to score only one or two goals in a game and sometimes no goals at all.*
   Ⓓ   *Some people believe this makes soccer boring to watch, but this is really what makes soccer so exciting.*

3   Where and when was the game of soccer invented? Write your answers on the lines.

   Where: _____   When: _____

4   What does the illustration mainly show about soccer?
   Ⓐ   How the field is set up
   Ⓑ   What the rules are for the goalkeeper
   Ⓒ   How players can use any part of their bodies
   Ⓓ   What the object of the game is

Alexander Graham Bell

Alexander Graham Bell is a famous inventor. He was born in Scotland in 1847. He is best known for inventing the telephone. His achievement was based on his research into hearing and speech. He was awarded a US patent for his invention in 1876. His telephone was quite different from those of today.

The following years saw his creation become used worldwide. Bell disliked the attention that his invention brought to him. Even though he invented it, he disliked telephones. He preferred to be left alone and not bothered. He did not even have a telephone in his place of work. He died in August, 1922.

Poor Elisha Gray

At the same time that Bell was developing his telephone, an inventor named Elisha Gray was developing his. Gray applied for a patent on his invention on the same day as Bell. However, Gray applied just a few short hours after Bell. Alexander Graham Bell was awarded the patent for the first telephone. If Elisha Gray had been a few hours quicker, he would be much more well known today.

CORE SKILLS PRACTICE

How do you think Elisha Gray would have felt when Alexander Graham Bell was awarded the patent for the first telephone? Explain your answer.

_____

_____

_____

_____

1 Which detail about Alexander Graham Bell would be least important to include in a summary of his life?

- Ⓐ He was born in Scotland in 1847.
- Ⓑ He is best known for inventing the telephone.
- Ⓒ He was awarded a patent for the telephone in 1876.
- Ⓓ He did not have a telephone in his place of work.

2 What type of passage is "Alexander Graham Bell"?

- Ⓐ Biography
- Ⓑ Autobiography
- Ⓒ Diary
- Ⓓ News article

3 Which detail given best explains why Bell disliked telephones?

- Ⓐ His telephone was different from those of today.
- Ⓑ Telephones became used all over the world.
- Ⓒ Bell liked to be left alone and not bothered.
- Ⓓ Bell did not have a telephone in his place of work.

4 Which sentence from "Poor Elisha Gray" suggests that Gray was unlucky?

- Ⓐ *At the same time that Bell was developing his telephone, an inventor named Elisha Gray was developing his.*
- Ⓑ *Gray applied for a patent on his invention on the same day as Bell.*
- Ⓒ *However, Gray applied just a few short hours after Bell.*
- Ⓓ *Alexander Graham Bell was awarded the patent for the first telephone.*

The First World War

The First World War was fought between 1914 and 1918. It was fought with Austria, Hungary, and Germany on one side. These countries were known as the Central Powers. England, France, and Russia were on the other side. These countries were known as the Allies. The United States joined the conflict in 1917. The United States joined the Allies. The German forces agreed to a ceasefire in November of that year.

First World War begins	The United States enters the war	First World War ends
July, 1914	April, 1917	November, 1918

CORE SKILLS PRACTICE

Summarize the information in the passage by completing the table below with the names of the countries that made up each group.

The Central Powers	The Allies

1 What does the timeline best show?

　Ⓐ　What caused the First World War

　Ⓑ　When the events of the war occurred

　Ⓒ　Why the United States entered the war

　Ⓓ　Where the main events of the war occurred

2 Where would this passage most likely be found?

　Ⓐ　In an encyclopedia

　Ⓑ　In an atlas

　Ⓒ　In a travel guide

　Ⓓ　In a book of short stories

3 What is the main purpose of the passage?

　Ⓐ　To instruct

　Ⓑ　To entertain

　Ⓒ　To persuade

　Ⓓ　To inform

4 The word <u>ceasefire</u> contains the word <u>cease</u>. What does the word <u>cease</u> mean?

　Ⓐ　Change

　Ⓑ　Grow

　Ⓒ　Stop

　Ⓓ　Upset

Camels

Camels can survive for long periods of time without drinking water. The camel's hump is a big help with this. But it does not actually store water. It stores fat. The fat is used as a source of energy. Many people forget that deserts are known for having little food as well as little water. By storing fat, camels can survive for weeks or even months without food. Camels do store water. They store it in their bodies and in their blood.

Camels can go longer than 7 days without drinking. When they do find water, they can take a lot in. They are able to consume over 50 gallons of water at a time! These features allow them to survive in the desert.

Camels were once found in North America. They are now mainly found in the deserts of the African and Arabian regions.

CORE SKILLS PRACTICE

This passage has three paragraphs. Each paragraph has a different topic. Describe the topic of each paragraph. The topic of the first paragraph has been completed for you.

Paragraph 1: What the purpose of a camel's hump is

Paragraph 2: _____

Paragraph 3: _____

1 When a camel drinks 50 gallons of water, where would the water most likely be stored?

- Ⓐ In its hump
- Ⓑ In its stomach
- Ⓒ In its blood
- Ⓓ In its skin

2 What type of passage is "Camels" most like?

- Ⓐ A short story
- Ⓑ A news article
- Ⓒ A magazine article
- Ⓓ An opinion piece

3 What is the main purpose of the passage?

- Ⓐ To describe what a camel's hump is for
- Ⓑ To explain how camels survive in deserts
- Ⓒ To tell where camels are found
- Ⓓ To show what camels look like

4 In which sentence does <u>store</u> mean the same as in the first paragraph?

- Ⓐ We <u>store</u> canned goods in the cellar.
- Ⓑ I went to the <u>store</u> to buy bread and milk.
- Ⓒ Hank dreamed of owning a sports <u>store</u> one day.
- Ⓓ There was a huge <u>store</u> of grain in the sheds.

5 Explain how a camel's hump helps it survive. Use information from the passage to support your answer.

Reading Comprehension

Set 10

Informational Texts

Instructions

Read each passage. Complete the exercise under each passage.

Then complete the questions following each passage. For each multiple-choice question, fill in the circle for the correct answer. For other types of questions, follow the instructions given. Some of the questions require a written answer. Write your answer on the lines provided.

Book Review

Sharon Creech's book *Love That Dog* is a creative story about a boy and poetry. *Love That Dog* is my favorite book because I am able to read a story in a special way. Instead of chapters, Sharon Creech organizes the book in short diary entries in the form of poems. The main character, Jack, learns how to write poetry and how to express his thoughts.

Throughout the book, Jack asks many questions about poetry. He often doesn't understand poems. However, Jack still copies the style in his own poetry. Eventually, Jack mentions the importance of a blue car when he writes a poem. After a while, Jack writes a full poem about the day his dog, Sky, got hit by a blue car. I can tell that it was difficult for Jack to write this poem because his teacher kept asking about the car and Jack did not want to explain at first. While the poem is sad, it was great that Jack was able to write it. Jack went from refusing to write poems and thinking that poetry was meaningless to writing an important poem about a difficult time in his life.

Love That Dog will always be a favorite book of mine. I was able to relate to the main character while also learning about poetry. It even encouraged me to try writing poetry of my own!

CORE SKILLS PRACTICE

In the first paragraph, the reviewer states that Jack learned "how to express his thoughts." Explain how the reviewer supports this statement in paragraph 2.

_____

_____

_____

_____

_____

1 According to the review, what makes Love That Dog creative?

- Ⓐ It is written in a unique style.
- Ⓑ It is based on an exciting plot.
- Ⓒ It tells of a sad event in a boy's life.
- Ⓓ It has a strong sense of mystery.

2 Which sentence from the first paragraph is organized by comparing and contrasting?

- Ⓐ *Sharon Creech's book* Love That Dog *is a creative story about a boy and poetry.*
- Ⓑ Love That Dog *is my favorite book because I am able to read a story in a special way.*
- Ⓒ *Instead of chapters, Sharon Creech organizes the book in short diary entries in the form of poems.*
- Ⓓ *The main character, Jack, learns how to write poetry and how to express his thoughts.*

3 Which sentence from the second paragraph gives the reviewer's opinion?

- Ⓐ *Throughout the book, Jack asks many questions about poetry.*
- Ⓑ *However, Jack still copies the style in his own poetry.*
- Ⓒ *After a while, Jack writes a full poem about the day his dog, Sky, got hit by a blue car.*
- Ⓓ *While the poem is sad, it was great that Jack was able to write it.*

4 In the last paragraph, what does the phrase "relate to" mean?

- Ⓐ Admire
- Ⓑ Copy
- Ⓒ Meet
- Ⓓ Understand

Beekeeping

Beekeeping was once best left to the professionals. The biggest problem was collecting the honey. Beekeepers had to wear special suits to avoid getting stung. Now, clever hives make it possible for everyone to keep bees. Collecting honey does not disturb the bees. It can be as simple as taking out a drawer, or even turning on a tap! Now everyone can take part in this useful hobby.

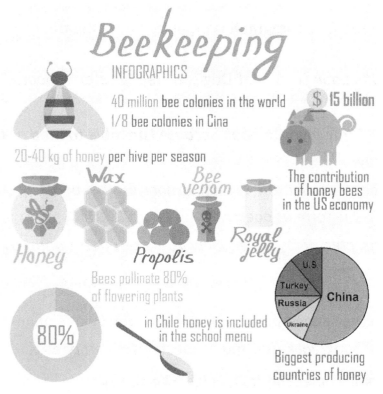

Modern beehive designs allow the honey to be collected without bothering the bees. Today, beekeepers do not need to be as careful as this person.

CORE SKILLS PRACTICE

What does the photograph in the passage show? Explain how it relates to the details in the passage.

_____

_____

_____

1 According to the poster, how much do honey bees add to the U.S. economy?

- Ⓐ $15 billion
- Ⓑ $20 billion
- Ⓒ $40 million
- Ⓓ $80 million

2 Which detail in the poster shows the importance of bees in nature?

- Ⓐ There are 40 million bee colonies in the world.
- Ⓑ A hive produces from 20 to 40 kilograms of honey each season.
- Ⓒ Bees pollinate 80 percent of flowering plants.
- Ⓓ Honey is included in the school menu in Chile.

3 Which of these describes the main idea of the paragraph in the passage?

- Ⓐ Beekeeping can be dangerous if you are not careful.
- Ⓑ Beekeeping is a great hobby for young people.
- Ⓒ Beekeeping is now easier and available to everyone.
- Ⓓ Beekeeping requires a lot of special equipment.

4 What does the circle graph on the poster show?

- Ⓐ The production of honey has increased over the years.
- Ⓑ Turkey produces some of the world's finest honey.
- Ⓒ Honey is a major part of the economy of the United States.
- Ⓓ Over half of the world's honey is produced in China.

Pizza Party Flyer

Dom's Italian Restaurant is turning 10 and we want all our loyal customers to celebrate with us!

Dom has been the proud owner for a decade now. He loves his customers and wants to give a little something back. Drop by and enjoy a free meal in a fun atmosphere. There will be plenty of free entertainment for the adults and the kids.

You can also check out our new menu and our new outdoor dining area.

Thank you for supporting us, and we look forward to providing the best Italian food in town for another 10 years.

CORE SKILLS PRACTICE

The passage states that the atmosphere of the party will be fun. What details on the flyer show why the atmosphere will be fun? Explain.

_____

_____

_____

_____

1 Which detail from the passage is a fact?

- Ⓐ Dom's Italian Restaurant is turning 10.
- Ⓑ The party will have a fun atmosphere.
- Ⓒ The restaurant provides the best Italian food in town.
- Ⓓ Dom loves and appreciates his customers.

2 Complete the list below to summarize the details of the pizza party.

Date: _____

Day: _____

Time: _____

Location: _____

3 Which detail from the flyer supports the statement that Dom wants to give something back?

- Ⓐ The organizer wants people to bring their friends.
- Ⓑ The party is being held at the restaurant.
- Ⓒ The restaurant is offering free pizza.
- Ⓓ The event takes place on the weekend.

4 According to the passage, what is the purpose of the pizza party?

- Ⓐ To attract new customers to the restaurant
- Ⓑ To honor the hard work of the owner
- Ⓒ To celebrate the restaurant's 10th birthday
- Ⓓ To introduce people to the new outdoor area

Yoga

Yoga can be tricky and challenging, but it doesn't have to be. You can start with simple poses and then move on to more difficult ones. But don't think that starting out simple means that it will not have benefits. Yoga is great for the mind and body and even basic poses have great health benefits. Yoga is suitable whether you are young or old. All you need to get started is some space and some free time. Just 30 minutes a day can leave you feeling refreshed.

CORE SKILLS PRACTICE

List **three** ways you can tell that the passage and poster is aimed at beginners.

1. _____

2. _____

3. _____

1 Which pose on the poster has details suggesting it is great for the mind? Select **all** the correct answers.

☐ Mountain Pose ☐ Downward-Facing Dog

☐ Warrior Pose ☐ Child's Pose

☐ Upward-Facing Dog

2 Which word best describes the overall tone of the poster?
- Ⓐ Concerned
- Ⓑ Encouraging
- Ⓒ Humble
- Ⓓ Serious

3 What is the main purpose of the list under each pose name?
- Ⓐ To encourage people to try each pose
- Ⓑ To ensure people use correct form for the pose
- Ⓒ To inform people about the history of the pose
- Ⓓ To summarize the benefits of the pose

4 Which detail from the first paragraph does the poster most strongly support?
- Ⓐ Yoga can be tricky and challenging.
- Ⓑ Even basic poses have great health benefits.
- Ⓒ Yoga is suitable whether you are young or old.
- Ⓓ Just 30 minutes a day can leave you feeling refreshed.

5 Write a letter for the school newspaper persuading students to try yoga. Use information from the passage to tell students why they should try yoga.

Reading Comprehension

Set 11

Literary and Informational Texts

Instructions

Read each passage. Complete the exercise under each passage.

Then complete the questions following each passage. For each multiple-choice question, fill in the circle for the correct answer. For other types of questions, follow the instructions given. Some of the questions require a written answer. Write your answer on the lines provided.

Herbal Tea

1. Add water to a kettle and wait until it has boiled.

2. Rinse the cup with boiling water to warm it up.

3. Place a teabag and a teaspoon or two of sugar (if required) in the cup.

4. Add the water and allow to sit for 90 seconds. You can let it sit for longer if you like your tea stronger.

5. Use a spoon to squeeze the tea bag. Then remove and stir the liquid.

6. If you like, you can add a dash of milk or cream.

If you are making tea for several people, follow the same steps but use a teapot instead of a cup.

> Did you know that herbal tea has many health benefits? People have been drinking herbal teas for centuries because of these benefits. You can choose the right type of tea to suit what you need.
>
> Peppermint tea can help you relax. Lemon tea can help a sore throat. Ginger tea can help calm a sore stomach. Chamomile tea can help you sleep.

CORE SKILLS PRACTICE

Describe **two** ways the information in the sidebar might influence a reader who is thinking about drinking herbal tea.

1. _____

2. _____

1   What is the meaning of the word <u>rinse</u> as used in the sentence below?

    Rinse the cup with boiling water to warm it up.

    Ⓐ   Scrub

    Ⓑ   Wash

    Ⓒ   Soak

    Ⓓ   Heat

2   What is the main purpose of the passage?

    Ⓐ   To teach readers how to make herbal tea

    Ⓑ   To tell about the history of herbal tea

    Ⓒ   To describe why herbal tea is popular

    Ⓓ   To persuade people to drink more herbal tea

3   Place the steps listed below in order from first to last. Write 1, 2, 3, and 4 on the lines to show the order.

    ____   Adding sugar

    ____   Adding milk or cream

    ____   Squeezing the tea bag

    ____   Rinsing the cup

4   In some of the steps, the maker can choose an action depending on how he or she wants the tea to taste. Circle **all** the steps that include a choice.

    Step 1   Step 2   Step 3

    Step 4   Step 5   Step 6

Fish Food

"Come on, it's not that far now!" Sam yelled.

Ben wiped away some sweat and kept going. It was a very warm day, and it just kept getting warmer.

Sam and Ben were on their way to the big lake to catch some fish. They had their fishing rods and some bait to put on their hooks.

They finally found a good spot near the lake. They sat down to start fishing. Ben opened the ice cream container where he had asked his mother to put the bait.

"This is not fishing bait. These worms are made of candy!" Ben said. "I should have told Mom I wanted worms to use as bait."

"We could still try," Sam offered. "Maybe the fish will like the candy worms."

Ben wasn't sure it would work, but it sounded like fun.

"It's worth a try," Ben said.

CORE SKILLS PRACTICE

The setting of a story is where and when it takes place. Sometimes a story will tell you the setting. Other times, you can guess the setting using details from the story. Answer the questions below about the setting of the story.

Where does this story take place? _____

What time of day do you think the story takes place? _____

What time of year do you think the story takes place? _____

1 What will Sam and Ben most likely do next?

　　Ⓐ　Start eating the candy worms

　　Ⓑ　Start fishing using the candy worms

　　Ⓒ　Choose a different spot to fish

　　Ⓓ　Decide to go home and do something else

2 What is the most likely reason Ben's mother put candy in the ice cream container?

　　Ⓐ　She thought that they would make good bait.

　　Ⓑ　She didn't realize that Ben wanted worms for bait.

　　Ⓒ　She didn't want Sam and Ben to catch any fish.

　　Ⓓ　She wanted Sam and Ben to have a snack to eat.

3 What happens right after Ben opens the ice cream container?

　　Ⓐ　He sees that he has candy worms.

　　Ⓑ　He finds a good fishing spot.

　　Ⓒ　He decides to fish anyway.

　　Ⓓ　He asks his mother to pack the bait.

4 What does Sam's reaction to seeing the candy worms suggest about his character?

　　Ⓐ　He gets angry easily.

　　Ⓑ　He sees the best in situations.

　　Ⓒ　He enjoys exciting activities.

　　Ⓓ　He is a good problem-solver.

The Capybara

There are approximately 2,200 species of rodents. Among the largest common rodents are beavers, squirrels, and chipmunks. However, most people associate the term rodent with rats or mice. The one thing that all rodents have in common is two pairs of front teeth that always grow. Rodents need to gnaw on plant material to keep these teeth short enough.

The largest rodent is the giant rat, or capybara. It can be found living in many countries in South America. The capybara can grow up to 4 feet long and can weigh anywhere between 75 and 150 pounds. They are mainly found near bodies of water, including in swamps. Capybaras are even found in the wetlands of Florida. Capybaras are herbivores and feed on plants, bark, and nuts.

CORE SKILLS PRACTICE

Capybaras are related to both mice and beavers. Do capybaras seem to have more in common with mice or beavers? Explain your answer.

_____

_____

_____

_____

_____

1 Complete the web below using information from the passage.

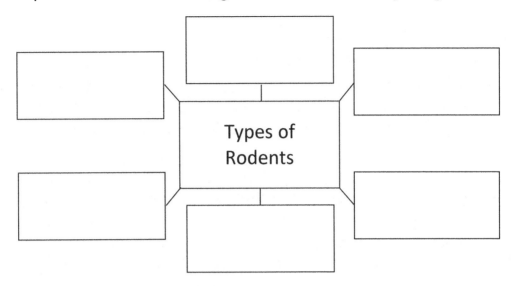

2 In the first paragraph, which word would best replace <u>associate</u>?

- Ⓐ Understand
- Ⓑ Organize
- Ⓒ Connect
- Ⓓ Imagine

3 The author probably wrote the passage mainly to –

- Ⓐ describe animals common to Florida
- Ⓑ compare and contrast different rodents
- Ⓒ give facts about one species of rodent
- Ⓓ convince readers that rodents are not pests

4 The tone of the passage is best described as –

- Ⓐ caring
- Ⓑ serious
- Ⓒ playful
- Ⓓ curious

The Light

Christopher woke up late one evening. He was drawn to a light shining in through his window. It was not bright enough to be blinding, but it seemed to shimmer. Christopher almost felt like it was dancing. It seemed to pulse and slide from one color into another. He hurried downstairs and out into the back garden. Something bright and dazzling glimmered in the sky above him. It seemed to be shining a spotlight on his home.

Christopher shielded his eyes as the strange craft moved towards him. It finally rested before him on the grass. It gave him a sense of calm that made any fear he had disappear. It seemed happy and welcoming. He thought he might have seen something just like it in a cartoon. As he stepped backwards, a door opened. A strange green outstretched arm welcomed him aboard. He paused, before stepping forward into the light.

CORE SKILLS PRACTICE

How does the author help the reader imagine the light in Christopher's room? In your answer, describe at least **two** details the author gives about the light.

_____

_____

_____

_____

_____

_____

_____

1 Read this sentence from the passage.

He was drawn to a light shining in through his window.

What does the phrase "drawn to" mean in the sentence?
- Ⓐ Shocked by
- Ⓑ Woken up by
- Ⓒ Attracted to
- Ⓓ Sketched

2 Which sentence shows Christopher's feelings about the events?
- Ⓐ *Christopher almost felt like it was dancing.*
- Ⓑ *Christopher shielded his eyes as the strange craft moved towards him.*
- Ⓒ *It gave him a sense of calm that made any fear he had disappear.*
- Ⓓ *He paused, before stepping forward into the light.*

3 The craft is described as "happy and welcoming." What does this help explain?
- Ⓐ Why the craft is shining
- Ⓑ What size the craft is
- Ⓒ Where the craft came from
- Ⓓ Why Christopher boarded the craft

4 What most likely caused Christopher to wake up?
- Ⓐ A loud noise
- Ⓑ A bright light
- Ⓒ A strange sight
- Ⓓ A bad dream

5 What do you think happens next in the passage? Use information from the passage to support your answer.

Reading Comprehension

Set 12

Literary and Informational Texts

Instructions

Read each passage. Complete the exercise under each passage.

Then complete the questions following each passage. For each multiple-choice question, fill in the circle for the correct answer. For other types of questions, follow the instructions given. Some of the questions require a written answer. Write your answer on the lines provided.

Thank You

Dear Grandma,

Thank you so much for the presents you sent me for my birthday! I am always amazed by how many wonderful things I receive. Of course, I had tried hard to be good all year. It is not easy to be good all the time, but I really tried hard. I have been polite and helpful to my friends and family.

This year, I got almost everything I asked for. This included a brand new bike. It is gold and sparkles like the Sun! I had wanted the puzzle you sent me for a long time as well. Thanks to you, I am going to try even harder to be good next year. I cannot wait for my birthday to come around again. I am already thinking about what to put on my birthday list for next year! I'm sure you'll find something special for me anyway. You always do!

Lots of love,

Lucy

CORE SKILLS PRACTICE

What main idea in the letter does the photograph mainly support?

_____

_____

_____

_____

_____

1 As it is used below, which word means the opposite of <u>polite</u>?

I have been polite and helpful to my friends and family.

- Ⓐ   Mean
- Ⓑ   Kind
- Ⓒ   Giving
- Ⓓ   Rude

2 Which sentence from the passage contains a simile?
- Ⓐ   *Thank you so much for the presents you sent me for my birthday!*
- Ⓑ   *This year, I got almost everything I asked for.*
- Ⓒ   *It is gold and sparkles like the Sun!*
- Ⓓ   *I cannot wait for my birthday to come around again.*

3 Which statement would Lucy most likely agree with?
- Ⓐ   Making the effort to be good was worth it.
- Ⓑ   She should have been given more presents.
- Ⓒ   It is not important to be nice to others.
- Ⓓ   It feels good to give presents to others.

4 Which sentence best shows that Lucy is grateful?
- Ⓐ   *I am always amazed by how many wonderful things I receive.*
- Ⓑ   *This year, I got almost everything I asked for.*
- Ⓒ   *I cannot wait for my birthday to come around again.*
- Ⓓ   *I am already thinking about what to put on my birthday list for next year!*

A Day in the Life

Jenny was very proud of her father. He was a local police officer. Jenny's father took great pride in protecting the people and keeping them safe. Jenny loved it when her father came home in the evening. He would talk about everything that happened that day. Jenny always had a million questions for him. She wanted to know absolutely everything about his day. She was amazed by how he seemed to handle everything that happened so well. His days were full of surprises, but he seemed ready for anything.

Sometimes he would tell how he tracked down a thief. Other times, he would describe how he directed traffic after an accident. Another day, he might tell how he pulled over people who were speeding. Some days, all he did was sit at his desk and do paperwork.

No matter what he told her, Jenny was always impressed. When she slept at night, Jenny would dream that one day she would be like her father.

CORE SKILLS PRACTICE

The author states that Jenny was "very proud of her father." What details does the author include to show how proud Jenny is?

_____

_____

_____

_____

_____

_____

1 Which words best show what protecting means?

> **Jenny's father took great pride in protecting the people and keeping them safe.**

- Ⓐ *Jenny's father*
- Ⓑ *great pride*
- Ⓒ *the people*
- Ⓓ *keeping them safe*

2 What is the second paragraph mainly about?
- Ⓐ The tasks that Jenny's father does
- Ⓑ Why Jenny wants to be a police officer
- Ⓒ What Jenny thinks of her father
- Ⓓ The problems that police officers have

3 Complete the table below using information from the passage.

Examples of Things that Jenny's Father Does at Work	
does paperwork	
pulls over speeding people	

4 Which sentence from the passage uses exaggeration?
- Ⓐ *Jenny was very proud of her father.*
- Ⓑ *He was a local police officer.*
- Ⓒ *Jenny loved it when her father came home in the evening.*
- Ⓓ *Jenny always had a million questions for him.*

Silver

Silver is a shiny metal. It is the best conductor of both heat and electricity. Even though it conducts electricity well, silver is not often used in wiring. Copper is used in wiring because it is far cheaper to buy. Silver is also the most reflective of all the metals. It is used in mirrors and other reflective coatings. It is also used in photographic film. The most common use of silver is industrial. Silver is used in solar panels and electronic devices such as cell phones.

Silver is often used to make jewelry, cutlery, and items like serving plates. Silver can even be used to sterilize water. This has been known for a very long time. The Persian king Cyrus the Great had his water supply boiled and sealed in silver vessels.

Silver is also used to make coins and medals. Quarters, dimes, and nickels are not made from silver, but investors can buy coins made of silver. Investors can also buy bars made of silver.

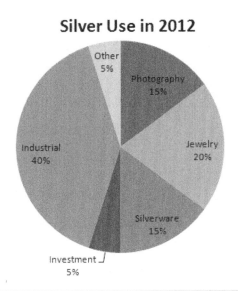

CORE SKILLS PRACTICE

Explain what the graph in the passage helps the reader understand.

_____

_____

_____

_____

_____

1 The passage says that copper is used in wiring because it is far cheaper to buy. Which word means the opposite of <u>cheaper</u>?

- Ⓐ Easier
- Ⓑ Harder
- Ⓒ Dearer
- Ⓓ Duller

2 Based on the passage, why is silver rarely used in electrical wiring?

- Ⓐ It has too many other uses.
- Ⓑ It does not conduct electricity.
- Ⓒ It heats up too much.
- Ⓓ It is too expensive.

3 If the passage were given another title, which title would best fit?

- Ⓐ The History of Silver
- Ⓑ The Silver Spoon
- Ⓒ The Many Uses of Silver
- Ⓓ How to Spot Silver

4 The word <u>reflective</u> is made up of the word <u>reflect</u> and the suffix <u>ive</u>. What does the word <u>reflective</u> mean?

- Ⓐ Able to reflect
- Ⓑ Cannot reflect
- Ⓒ One who reflects
- Ⓓ The state of reflecting

Creature Comforts

Fred the farmer loved his job. He enjoyed nothing more than waking up at sunrise to feed and tend to his animals. He would even sing to them as he visited them in the morning. Even during the cold days of winter, he never once complained. He just put on thick socks and an extra coat and went out into the freezing cold air. The wind whipped around him and tried to annoy him. But Fred just focused on his tasks. On many cold days, it was almost dark by the time he had finished all his work and was able to go home to have dinner and rest. He was too tired by then to do much, so he would make himself a quick and easy dinner. After eating, he would just sit back and relax before going to bed ready for the next early morning.

When the summer sun rose high in the sky and the day became very hot, he still loved working hard. There was always something that had to be done on the farm. There were fences to be fixed, wire on the hen house to be hatched, or bales of hay to deliver to the horses. He was always pleased knowing that he was making his animals happy and comfortable. Although they couldn't speak, Fred knew that his animals were happy with their life on his farm.

CORE SKILLS PRACTICE

Explain whether or not you think Fred is happy and content.

_____

_____

_____

_____

_____

1   Read this sentence from the passage.

> **He enjoyed nothing more than waking up at sunrise to feed and tend to his animals.**

What does the phrase "tend to" mean?

- Ⓐ   Give water
- Ⓑ   Sing to
- Ⓒ   Look after
- Ⓓ   Spend time with

2   What does the title of the passage suggest?

- Ⓐ   That the animals on the farm are happy
- Ⓑ   That Fred the farmer works too hard
- Ⓒ   That many animals live on farms
- Ⓓ   That animals make life easier

3   Which word best describes Fred?

- Ⓐ   Kind
- Ⓑ   Careless
- Ⓒ   Impatient
- Ⓓ   Amusing

4   Which sentence best supports your answer to Question 3?

- Ⓐ   *He would even sing to them as he visited them in the morning.*
- Ⓑ   *Even during the cold days of winter, he never once complained.*
- Ⓒ   *The wind whipped around him and tried to annoy him.*
- Ⓓ   *He was always pleased knowing that he was making his animals happy and comfortable.*

5 How does the author show that life on the farm is hard? Use information from the passage to support your answer.

Reading Comprehension

Set 13

Paired Literary Texts

Instructions

This set contains a pair of passages. Read each passage on its own first. Complete the exercise under each passage. Then complete the questions following each passage.

For each multiple-choice question, fill in the circle for the correct answer. For other types of questions, follow the instructions given. Some of the questions require a written answer. Write your answer on the lines provided.

After reading both passages, you will answer one or more additional questions. You will use information from both passages to answer these questions. Write your answers on the lines provided.

Soccer

Molly loved soccer. Her two older brothers both played all the time. Whenever her brothers practiced, she always joined in and gave it her all. Ever since she was young, she had joined in with them when they played in the park. They had taught her how to tackle a player well, how to head the ball into the goal, and how to strike the ball with force. She was never quite as good as they were, but she practiced often and got better and better.

One day the coach of her school's soccer team had to choose a team to play against another local school. Molly was watching from the side hoping that her brothers would be picked. Then the coach pointed to her and motioned for her to come over. He explained that she was his first pick for the team. He had seen her playing and was impressed with her skills. Molly could hardly believe it. She would be the only girl on the team. Her brothers were surprised too, but they were happy for her. They were even happier when they were picked as well. Molly was looking forward to training with them as part of a real team.

CORE SKILLS PRACTICE

The title of this passage is "Soccer." A better title for the passage would describe the message of the passage. Think of a new title for the passage. Write the title below, and then explain why it would be a good title for the passage.

Title: _____

_____

_____

_____

_____

_____

1   In this sentence, what does the phrase "gave it her all" show about Molly?

> **Whenever her brothers practiced, she always joined in and gave it her all.**

- Ⓐ She gave the boys a gift.
- Ⓑ She was not good at soccer.
- Ⓒ She tried very hard.
- Ⓓ She scored many points.

2   What is the most likely reason Molly did not expect to be picked?
- Ⓐ She is female.
- Ⓑ She does not know how to play.
- Ⓒ She is not old enough.
- Ⓓ She loves playing soccer.

3   How does Molly most likely feel about being picked for the team?
- Ⓐ Shocked and scared
- Ⓑ Surprised, but happy
- Ⓒ Confused and annoyed
- Ⓓ Excited, but worried

4   How does the information in the first paragraph help explain why Molly was picked for the team?
- Ⓐ It explains why she enjoys playing soccer so much.
- Ⓑ It shows how playing with her brothers gave her good skills.
- Ⓒ It explains that she has a natural talent for soccer.
- Ⓓ It shows that she is a determined person who gets what she wants.

5 How do the brothers in the passage support Molly? In your answer, describe at least **two** details given that show that they support her.

Something Special

Toby had played basketball for the school since he was eleven. When he reached sixteen, he was dropped from the team because his coach said he was too short. Toby was upset, but his father told him not to give up. He told him to keep playing and enjoying the game.

Toby played on the weekend with his friends. After school, he played by himself. Without anyone else to play with, he spent a lot of time learning ball skills. He enjoyed learning to do new things with the ball. But he missed playing in real games and being part of a team.

When they moved the following year, Toby trained with his new school team. His coach was impressed with his ball skills. Toby was delighted to be selected for the team. He later became the star player for his new team.

CORE SKILLS PRACTICE

This story is written from a third person point of view. This means it is written by someone who is not part of the story. Now imagine that the story is written from Toby's point of view. Write a paragraph from Toby's point of view describing being dropped from the team.

_____

_____

_____

_____

_____

6 How does being dropped from the school team help Toby?

- Ⓐ He improves his ball skills.
- Ⓑ He decides to move.
- Ⓒ He gets other interests.
- Ⓓ He becomes upset.

7 What type of passage is "Something Special"?

- Ⓐ Realistic fiction
- Ⓑ Biography
- Ⓒ Science fiction
- Ⓓ Fable

8 What is Toby's main problem in the passage?

- Ⓐ He cannot play on the school basketball team.
- Ⓑ His friends are too busy to play with him.
- Ⓒ He is moving to a new school.
- Ⓓ He is chosen for a basketball team after he moves.

9 In the last paragraph, the word <u>delighted</u> shows that Toby was –

- Ⓐ very angry
- Ⓑ very pleased
- Ⓒ very surprised
- Ⓓ very confused

Directions: Use both passages to answer the following questions.

10 Compare how Molly feels about playing soccer with how Toby feels about playing basketball.

11 Describe how Molly and Toby develop strong sporting skills. In what way is the way they develop skills similar?

12 At the end of each passage, Molly and Toby are chosen to play on a sports team. Describe how they each feel about being chosen and why they feel that way.

Reading Comprehension

Set 14

Paired Informational Texts

Instructions

This set contains a pair of passages. Read each passage on its own first. Complete the exercise under each passage. Then complete the questions following each passage.

For each multiple-choice question, fill in the circle for the correct answer. For other types of questions, follow the instructions given. Some of the questions require a written answer. Write your answer on the lines provided.

After reading both passages, you will answer one or more additional questions. You will use information from both passages to answer these questions. Write your answers on the lines provided.

Brain Size

Did you know that the common ant has the largest brain in relation to its size? Of course, an ant's brain is much smaller than a human's brain. But the brain of an ant is 6 percent of its total body weight. The average human brain is just over 2 percent of a person's body weight.

A single ant brain has a fraction of the ability of a human one. But a colony of ants may have just as much ability. An average nest has 40,000 ants. In total, these ants would have about the same number of brain cells as a person.

Ants are known for their ability to work together. In a colony, ants have different roles. Some build the nest, some seek out food, and others protect the nest. Ants communicate with each other using sounds, touch, and special chemicals they release.

CORE SKILLS PRACTICE

List **three** differences between the brain of an ant and the brain of a human.

1. _____

_____

2. _____

_____

3. _____

_____

1	Where would this passage most likely be found?
	Ⓐ	In a science magazine
	Ⓑ	In a book of short stories
	Ⓒ	In an encyclopedia
	Ⓓ	In a travel guide

2	Why does the author begin the passage with a question?
	Ⓐ	To get readers interested in the topic of the passage
	Ⓑ	To show that the information may not be correct
	Ⓒ	To suggest that readers should research the topic
	Ⓓ	To indicate that there are facts to support the idea

3	According to the passage, how many ants are equal to one human brain?
	Ⓐ	2
	Ⓑ	6
	Ⓒ	20,000
	Ⓓ	40,000

4	What does the photograph in the passage represent?
	Ⓐ	Ants communicating with each other
	Ⓑ	Ants protecting a nest
	Ⓒ	Ants working together
	Ⓓ	Ants having different roles

Ants Seeking Food

You're hungry and you need to find food. How do you find a grocery store or a restaurant? You might look it up on a computer or a phone. You might ask someone if they know where you can get something to eat nearby. You might look for signs and follow those. This is something like what ants do to find food.

When an ant finds a source of food, it leaves a trail on its way back to the nest. It makes the trail by releasing chemicals that other ants can sense. Another ant will sense the chemicals and follow the trail. On the way back, that ant will release more chemicals. The trail will become stronger as more ants follow the trail. It's like what happens when people walk through the woods. When just one person walks a path, the trail is hard to spot. But as more and more people follow the same path, the trail gets more noticeable. The more noticeable the trail, the more people walk it. Ants act the same way. Eventually, there will be an army of ants marching the strong trail that has been created.

Before long, the food source will run out. The ants will no longer release chemicals on their way back. The trail will begin to fade. The ants will move on to find a new path to follow to food. Luckily, there are always ants out looking for food, so new paths are being created all the time.

CORE SKILLS PRACTICE

Why do you think the author begins the passage by asking how people find food?

_____

_____

_____

_____

_____

5   In the sentence below, what does the phrase "army of ants" show?

   Eventually, there will be an army of ants marching the strong trail that has been created.

   Ⓐ   The ants will fight over the food.
   Ⓑ   There will be a large number of ants.
   Ⓒ   The ants are well-organized.
   Ⓓ   The ants will all follow the same path.

6   Why does the author describe people walking through the woods in the second paragraph?

   Ⓐ   To inform readers about where ant trails can be found
   Ⓑ   To suggest that people should help each other like ants do
   Ⓒ   To help readers understand how trails get stronger
   Ⓓ   To explain that ant trails are not easy to see

7   Which sentence from the passage describes a cause and effect?

   Ⓐ   *How do you find a grocery store or a restaurant?*
   Ⓑ   *This is something like what ants do to find food.*
   Ⓒ   *On the way back, that ant will release more chemicals.*
   Ⓓ   *The more noticeable the trail, the more people walk it.*

8   Which sentence is best supported by the information in the passage?

   Ⓐ   Ants are helpful to each other.
   Ⓑ   Ants have lots of energy.
   Ⓒ   Ants harm the environment.
   Ⓓ   Ants are selfish creatures.

Directions: Use both passages to answer the following question.

9   Ants are referred to as social creatures because they work together and communicate with each other. Use details from both passages to explain how and why ants work together.

ANSWER KEY

Common Core State Standards

The state of California has adopted the Common Core State Standards. These standards describe what students are expected to know. Student learning throughout the year is based on these standards, and all the questions on the state tests assess these standards.

All the exercises and questions in this book cover the Common Core State Standards. This book will develop all the Common Core reading skills, as well as complementary writing and language skills.

Core Skills Practice

Each passage includes an exercise focused on one key skill described in the Common Core standards. The answer key identifies the core skill covered by each exercise, and describes what to look for in the student's response.

Common Core Reading Standards

The Common Core reading standards are divided into the following two areas:

- Reading Standards for Literature
- Reading Standards for Informational Text

Within each of these areas, there are nine standards that describe specific skills the student should have. The answer key on the following pages lists the standard assessed by each question. The skill listed can be used to identify a student's areas of strength and weakness, so revision and instruction can be targeted accordingly.

Scoring Constructed-Response Questions

This workbook includes constructed-response questions, where students provide a written answer to a question. Short questions are scored out of 2 and longer questions are scored out of 4. The answer key gives guidance on how to score these questions. Use the criteria listed as a guide to scoring these questions, and as a guide for giving the student advice on how to improve an answer.

Set 1: Literary Texts

The Acorn

Core Skills Practice

Core skill: Describe a character and event in a story

Answer: The student should explain that the man decides that acorns should grow on trees and pumpkins should grow on the ground when the acorn falls on his head. The answer should show an understanding of how the man realizes that it would be a problem if pumpkins grew on trees because they would fall on people and hurt them.

Question	Answer	Common Core Reading Standard
1	B	Determine a theme of a story, drama, or poem from details in the text; summarize the text.
2	D	Determine the meaning of words and phrases as they are used in a text, including those that allude to significant characters found in mythology.
3	C	Make connections between the text of a story or drama and a visual or oral presentation of the text, identifying where each version reflects specific descriptions and directions in the text.
4	A	Compare and contrast the point of view from which different stories are narrated, including the difference between first- and third-person narrations.

Tom's Time Machine

Core Skills Practice

Core skill: Write a narrative

Answer: The student should write a paragraph that continues the story.

Question	Answer	Common Core Reading Standard
1	B	Make connections between the text of a story or drama and a visual or oral presentation of the text, identifying where each version reflects specific descriptions and directions in the text.
2	A	Explain major differences between poems, drama, and prose, and refer to the structural elements of poems and drama when writing or speaking about a text.
3	C	Describe in depth a character, setting, or event in a story or drama, drawing on specific details in the text.
4	B	Determine the meaning of words and phrases as they are used in a text, including those that allude to significant characters found in mythology.

Making Mistakes

Core Skills Practice

Core skill: Describe how a character changes in a text

Answer: The student should identify that Kelly is upset or annoyed in the first paragraph and calmer in the last paragraph. The student should describe how Kelly does better when she is calm.

Question	Answer	Common Core Reading Standard
1	D	Refer to details and examples in a text when explaining what the text says explicitly and when drawing inferences from the text.
2	C	Make connections between the text of a story or drama and a visual or oral presentation of the text, identifying where each version reflects specific descriptions and directions in the text.
3	B	Describe in depth a character, setting, or event in a story or drama, drawing on specific details in the text.
4	A	Determine a theme of a story, drama, or poem from details in the text; summarize the text.

In the End

Core Skills Practice

Core skill: Compare and contract characters

Answer: The student should describe how Michael runs fast, while Stephen keeps a steady pace.

Question	Answer	Common Core Reading Standard
1	B	Determine the meaning of words and phrases as they are used in a text, including those that allude to significant characters found in mythology.
2	A	Determine a theme of a story, drama, or poem from details in the text; summarize the text.
3	B	Explain major differences between poems, drama, and prose, and refer to the structural elements of poems and drama when writing or speaking about a text.
4	C	Explain major differences between poems, drama, and prose, and refer to the structural elements of poems and drama when writing or speaking about a text.
5	See Below	Describe in depth a character, setting, or event in a story or drama, drawing on specific details in the text.

Give a score of 0, 1, 2, 3, or 4 based on how well the answer meets the criteria listed.
- It should make a valid inference about how Michael feels after the race, such as that he feels upset, disappointed, or determined to do better next time.
- It should include a fully-supported explanation of why the student believes this.
- It should use relevant details from the passage.
- It should be well-organized, clear, and easy to understand.

Set 2: Informational Texts

The Rubik's Cube

Core Skills Practice

Core skill: Explain how authors use reasons to support particular points

Answer: The student should explain how the last paragraph supports the idea that once you learn to solve the puzzle, the fun is just beginning. The answer should refer to how you can keep trying to solve it faster or try to solve it in different ways.

Question	Answer	Common Core Reading Standard
1	created invented	Determine the meaning of general academic and domain-specific words or phrases in a text relevant to a grade 4 topic or subject area.
2	D	Explain how an author uses reasons and evidence to support particular points in a text.
3	F, O, F, F, O, F	Compare and contrast a firsthand and secondhand account of the same event or topic; describe the differences in focus and the information provided.
4	B	Explain events, procedures, ideas, or concepts in a historical, scientific, or technical text, including what happened and why, based on specific information in the text.

Big Ben

Core Skills Practice

Core skill: Summarize key information in a text

Answer: The student should answer the questions based on the information in the passage.
- Big Ben is in the United Kingdom.
- Big Ben is in the Palace of Westminster.
- Big Ben was built in 1858.
- Big Ben celebrated its 150th anniversary in 2009.

Question	Answer	Common Core Reading Standard
1	B	Determine the meaning of general academic and domain-specific words or phrases in a text relevant to a grade 4 topic or subject area.
2	A	Determine the main idea of a text and explain how it is supported by key details; summarize the text.
3	C	Compare and contrast a firsthand and secondhand account of the same event or topic; describe the differences in focus and the information provided.
4	A	Determine the meaning of general academic and domain-specific words or phrases in a text relevant to a grade 4 topic or subject area.

Sir Isaac Newton

Core Skills Practice
Core skill: Write an informative text
Answer: The student should list questions that would be appropriate to answer in a report.

Question	Answer	Common Core Reading Standard
1	C	Determine the meaning of general academic and domain-specific words or phrases in a text relevant to a grade 4 topic or subject area.
2	C	Describe the overall structure (e.g., chronology, comparison, cause/effect, problem/solution) of events, ideas, concepts, or information in a text or part of a text.
3	D	Refer to details and examples in a text when explaining what the text says explicitly and when drawing inferences from the text.
4	B	Interpret information presented visually, orally, or quantitatively and explain how the information contributes to an understanding of the text in which it appears.

Mount Mauna Kea

Core Skills Practice
Core skill: Explain how information presented visually adds to a text
Answer: The student should describe a diagram that shows the heights of Mount Everest and Mount Mauna Kea.

Question	Answer	Common Core Reading Standard
1	D	Determine the meaning of general academic and domain-specific words or phrases in a text relevant to a grade 4 topic or subject area.
2	D	Determine the main idea of a text and explain how it is supported by key details; summarize the text.
3	B	Determine the main idea of a text and explain how it is supported by key details; summarize the text.
4	A	Interpret information presented visually, orally, or quantitatively and explain how the information contributes to an understanding of the text in which it appears.
5	See Below	Explain events, procedures, ideas, or concepts in a historical, scientific, or technical text, including what happened and why, based on specific information in the text.

Give a score of 0, 1, 2, 3, or 4 based on how well the answer meets the criteria listed.
- It should identify how Mount Everest and Mount Mauna Kea are similar.
- It should identify how Mount Everest and Mount Mauna Kea are different.
- It should use relevant details from the passage.
- It should be well-organized, clear, and easy to understand.

Set 3: Informational Texts

Advertisement

Core Skills Practice

Core skill: Form and express an opinion based on a text

Answer: The student should state whether or not he or she would choose the product for breakfast. The student should use details from the advertisement to explain the choice.

Question	Answer	Common Core Reading Standard
1	C	Determine the meaning of general academic and domain-specific words or phrases in a text relevant to a grade 4 topic or subject area.
2	D	Explain how an author uses reasons and evidence to support particular points in a text.
3	B	Interpret information presented visually, orally, or quantitatively and explain how the information contributes to an understanding of the text in which it appears.
4	D	Refer to details and examples in a text when explaining what the text says explicitly and when drawing inferences from the text.

Bacon Sandwich

Core Skills Practice

Core skill: Use context to determine the meaning of words and phrases

Answer: The student should explain what the phrase "add your own twist" means. The answer should refer to adding something different to the sandwich or making it in a unique or individual way.

Question	Answer	Common Core Reading Standard
1	D	Determine the meaning of general academic and domain-specific words or phrases in a text relevant to a grade 4 topic or subject area.
2	A	Refer to details and examples in a text when explaining what the text says explicitly and when drawing inferences from the text.
3	2 bacon 4 cheese 3 bread 1 oil	Explain events, procedures, ideas, or concepts in a historical, scientific, or technical text, including what happened and why, based on specific information in the text.
4	B	Integrate information from two texts on the same topic in order to write or speak about the subject knowledgeably.

Monarch Butterflies

Core Skills Practice

Core skill: Explain how a main idea is supported by key details / Summarize a text

Answer: The student should summarize the three reasons below.
- They migrate each year.
- They need milkweed plants to survive.
- They have been into space.

Question	Answer	Common Core Reading Standard
1	B	Determine the meaning of general academic and domain-specific words or phrases in a text relevant to a grade 4 topic or subject area.
2	C	Integrate information from two texts on the same topic in order to write or speak about the subject knowledgeably.
3	C	Describe the overall structure of events, ideas, concepts, or information in a text or part of a text.
4	A	Interpret information presented visually, orally, or quantitatively and explain how the information contributes to an understanding of the text in which it appears.

Monument Valley

Core Skills Practice

Core skill: Determine the meaning of words and phrases in a text

Answer: The student should explain what the phrase "a well-known icon of the American Southwest" means. The answer should refer to how the area represents the American Southwest because of its unique features.

Question	Answer	Common Core Reading Standard
1	C	Interpret information presented visually, orally, or quantitatively and explain how the information contributes to an understanding of the text in which it appears.
2	A	Describe the overall structure of events, ideas, concepts, or information in a text or part of a text.
3	B	Interpret information presented visually, orally, or quantitatively and explain how the information contributes to an understanding of the text in which it appears.
4	A	Refer to details and examples in a text when explaining what the text says explicitly and when drawing inferences from the text.
5	See Below	Refer to details and examples in a text when explaining what the text says explicitly and when drawing inferences from the text.

Give a score of 0, 1, 2, 3, or 4 based on how well the answer meets the criteria listed.
- It should give a reasonable explanation of what attracts people to the park.
- It may refer to the beauty, the activities, or the culture.
- It should use relevant details from the passage.
- It should be well-organized, clear, and easy to understand.

Set 4: Literary and Informational Texts

The Basement Door

Core Skills Practice

Core skill: Describe a setting, drawing on specific details in a text

Answer: The student should identify two details that make the basement seem creepy and explain how they make the basement seem creepy. The answer could refer to the creaking door, the complete darkness, the cold air, or the faded wooden stairs.

Question	Answer	Common Core Reading Standard
1	C	Describe in depth a character, setting, or event in a story or drama, drawing on specific details in the text.
2	D	Determine a theme of a story, drama, or poem from details in the text; summarize the text.
3	C	Determine the meaning of words and phrases as they are used in a text, including those that allude to significant characters found in mythology.
4	sound sight touch	Explain major differences between poems, drama, and prose, and refer to the structural elements of poems and drama when writing or speaking about a text.

The Olympics

Core Skills Practice

Core skill: Write an opinion piece

Answer: The student should give an opinion on whether or not winning an Olympic medal is a worthwhile goal, and should support the opinion with a valid explanation.

Question	Answer	Common Core Reading Standard
1	A	Compare and contrast a firsthand and secondhand account of the same event or topic; describe the differences in focus and the information provided.
2	B	Determine the meaning of general academic and domain-specific words or phrases in a text relevant to a grade 4 topic or subject area.
3	B	Determine the meaning of general academic and domain-specific words or phrases in a text relevant to a grade 4 topic or subject area.
4	D	Interpret information presented visually, orally, or quantitatively and explain how the information contributes to an understanding of the text in which it appears.

Air

Core Skills Practice

Core skill: Interpret information presented visually

Answer: The student should explain that the photograph helps show how nitrogen is added to the air by volcanoes.

Question	Answer	Common Core Reading Standard
1	C	Describe the overall structure (e.g., chronology, comparison, cause/effect, problem/solution) of events, ideas, concepts, or information in a text or part of a text.
2	4, 3, 1, 2	Explain events, procedures, ideas, or concepts in a historical, scientific, or technical text, including what happened and why, based on specific information in the text.
3	B	Interpret information presented visually, orally, or quantitatively and explain how the information contributes to an understanding of the text in which it appears.
4	C	Describe the overall structure (e.g., chronology, comparison, cause/effect, problem/solution) of events, ideas, concepts, or information in a text or part of a text.

Visiting the Circus

Core Skills Practice

Core skill: Describe in depth a character based on a character's thoughts, words, or actions

Answer: The student may describe how Mickey feels nervous, how Mickey froze when the clowns came out, how Mickey told himself not to be afraid, or how Mickey's hands shook.

Question	Answer	Common Core Reading Standard
1	C	Determine the meaning of words and phrases as they are used in a text, including those that allude to significant characters found in mythology.
2	A	Determine a theme of a story, drama, or poem from details in the text; summarize the text.
3	B	Describe in depth a character, setting, or event in a story or drama, drawing on specific details in the text.
4	D	Compare and contrast the point of view from which different stories are narrated, including the difference between first- and third-person narrations.
5	See Below	Refer to details and examples in a text when explaining what the text says explicitly and when drawing inferences from the text.

Give a score of 0, 1, 2, 3, or 4 based on how well the answer meets the criteria listed.
- It should provide a well-supported argument about why Mickey can be considered brave.
- It should use relevant details from the passage.
- It should be well-organized, clear, and easy to understand.

Set 5: Literary and Informational Texts

Beneath the Stars

Core Skills Practice

Core skill: Refer to details in a text when drawing inferences from the text

Answer: The student should identify that the family spend more time together or more time talking because they do not have television or computers. The student should explain that Brian enjoys camping because he gets to chat with his family more.

Question	Answer	Common Core Reading Standard
1	D	Make connections between the text of a story or drama and a visual or oral presentation of the text, identifying where each version reflects specific descriptions and directions in the text.
2	D	Describe in depth a character, setting, or event in a story or drama, drawing on specific details in the text.
3	C	Refer to details and examples in a text when explaining what the text says explicitly and when drawing inferences from the text.
4	C	Determine the meaning of words and phrases as they are used in a text, including those that allude to significant characters found in mythology.

The Dodo

Core Skills Practice

Core skill: Explain events in a text, including what happened and why

Answer: The student should explain why the dodo became extinct. The reasons included may be that animals started eating the eggs, that people started hunting the dodos, and that the forests where the dodos lived started to be destroyed.

Question	Answer	Common Core Reading Standard
1	A	Describe the overall structure (e.g., chronology, comparison, cause/effect, problem/solution) of events, ideas, concepts, or information in a text or part of a text.
2	D	Explain events, procedures, ideas, or concepts in a historical, scientific, or technical text, including what happened and why, based on specific information in the text.
3	C	Refer to details and examples in a text when explaining what the text says explicitly and when drawing inferences from the text.
4	D	Determine the meaning of general academic and domain-specific words or phrases in a text relevant to a grade 4 topic or subject area.

Dearest Donna

Core Skills Practice
Core skill: Identify the audience and purpose of a text
Answer: The student should identify that the audience is Donna, or the author's girlfriend. The student should explain that the poet wrote the poem to express his love.

Question	Answer	Common Core Reading Standard
1	D	Explain major differences between poems, drama, and prose, and refer to the structural elements of poems and drama when writing or speaking about a text.
2	D	Explain major differences between poems, drama, and prose, and refer to the structural elements of poems and drama when writing or speaking about a text.
3	C	Determine the meaning of words and phrases as they are used in a text, including those that allude to significant characters found in mythology.
4	A	Determine a theme of a story, drama, or poem from details in the text; summarize the text.

Letter to the Editor

Core Skills Practice
Core skill: Explain how authors use reasons to support particular points
Answer: The student should identify the details used to show that the park is not inviting. These include the overflowing trash cans, the unmowed grass, the trash, and the graffiti.

Question	Answer	Common Core Reading Standard
1	C	Refer to details and examples in a text when explaining what the text says explicitly and when drawing inferences from the text.
2	B	Determine the main idea of a text and explain how it is supported by key details; summarize the text.
3	B	Determine the meaning of general academic and domain-specific words or phrases in a text relevant to a grade 4 topic or subject area.
4	D	Compare and contrast a firsthand and secondhand account of the same event or topic; describe the differences in focus and the information provided.
5	See Below	Explain how an author uses reasons and evidence to support particular points in a text.

Give a score of 0, 1, 2, 3, or 4 based on how well the answer meets the criteria listed.
- It should give at least two examples of how the poor state of the park is affecting people.
- The effects could include that people are not taking their kids to the park, that people are not walking their dogs, that people do not feel safe, or that people cannot use it happily.
- It should use relevant details from the passage.
- It should be well-organized, clear, and easy to understand.

Set 6: Paired Literary Texts

Peace and Not War/The Waggiest Tail

Core Skills Practice
Core skill: Describe in depth a setting in a story
Answer: The student should describe how saying the living room sounds like a zoo shows how noisy it was. The student should give a reasonable explanation of whether this description helps readers imagine the scene.

Core Skills Practice
Core skill: Draw inferences from a text
Answer: The student may describe how the use of the words adds humor to the passage, or how it helps show how silly the argument is.

Question	Answer	Common Core Reading Standard
1	B	Describe in depth a character, setting, or event in a story or drama, drawing on specific details in the text.
2	C	Refer to details and examples in a text when explaining what the text says explicitly and when drawing inferences from the text.
3	B	Determine a theme of a story, drama, or poem from details in the text; summarize the text.
4	B	Determine the meaning of words and phrases as they are used in a text, including those that allude to significant characters found in mythology.
5	B	Explain major differences between poems, drama, and prose, and refer to the structural elements of poems and drama when writing or speaking about a text.
6	C	Determine a theme of a story, drama, or poem from details in the text; summarize the text.
7	C	Refer to details and examples in a text when explaining what the text says explicitly and when drawing inferences from the text.
8	A	Describe in depth a character, setting, or event in a story or drama, drawing on specific details in the text.
9	See Below	Determine a theme of a story, drama, or poem from details in the text; summarize the text.
10	See Below	Compare and contrast the treatment of similar themes and topics and patterns of events in stories, myths, and traditional literature from different cultures.
11	See Below	Compare and contrast the treatment of similar themes and topics and patterns of events in stories, myths, and traditional literature from different cultures.
12	See Below	Determine a theme of a story, drama, or poem from details in the text; summarize the text.

Q9.
Give a score of 0, 1, 2, 3, or 4 based on how well the answer meets the criteria listed.
- It should describe how the author wants readers to learn that it is silly to argue with a friend about something that is not important.
- It should use relevant details from the passage.
- It should be well-organized, clear, and easy to understand.

Q10.
Give a score of 0, 1, or 2 based on how well the answer meets the criteria listed.
- It should describe similarities or differences between the mothers in the two passages.
- The answer may identify that they both find the fights silly or that one mother is more harsh than the other.
- It should refer to how the mother in "Peace and Not War" is more upset with the fighting.

Q11.
Give a score of 0, 1, or 2 based on how well the answer meets the criteria listed.
- It should identify that the problem is not solved in "Peace and Not War" because the brothers continue to fight.
- It should identify that the problem is solved in "The Waggiest Tail" because the girls realize that their fight is silly.

Q12.
Give a score of 0, 1, 2, 3, or 4 based on how well the answer meets the criteria listed.
- It should identify the main lesson of the passages as being about not arguing about silly things, about recognizing what is important, or about learning to get along.
- It should include a reasonable description of how the student could apply the lesson.
- It should use relevant details from both passages.
- It should be well-organized, clear, and easy to understand.

Set 7: Paired Informational Texts

Pompeii/Volcanoes

Core Skills Practice

Core skill: Explain how authors use reasons to support particular points

Answer: The student should list two facts that show how powerful the eruption was. The facts could include that it was the largest of all time, that 1.5 million tons of lava flowed out per second, that material was thrown into the air and reached heights of over 20 miles, or that 4 meters of ash covered Pompeii.

Core Skills Practice

Core skill: Contrast two items / Explain concepts in a scientific text

Answer: The student should explain that magma is below the surface of the Earth and lava is above the surface of the Earth.

Question	Answer	Common Core Reading Standard
1	B	Determine the meaning of general academic and domain-specific words or phrases in a text relevant to a grade 4 topic or subject area.
2	C	Describe the overall structure (e.g., chronology, comparison, cause/effect, problem/solution) of events, ideas, concepts, or information in a text or part of a text.
3	A	Determine the main idea of a text and explain how it is supported by key details; summarize the text.
4	C	Compare and contrast a firsthand and secondhand account of the same event or topic; describe the differences in focus and the information provided.
5	C	Describe the overall structure (e.g., chronology, comparison, cause/effect, problem/solution) of events, ideas, concepts, or information in a text or part of a text.
6	D	Determine the meaning of general academic and domain-specific words or phrases in a text relevant to a grade 4 topic or subject area.
7	B	Refer to details and examples in a text when explaining what the text says explicitly and when drawing inferences from the text.
8	B	Interpret information presented visually, orally, or quantitatively and explain how the information contributes to an understanding of the text in which it appears.
9	See Below	Integrate information from two texts on the same topic in order to write or speak about the subject knowledgeably.

Q9.
Give a score of 0, 1, 2, 3, or 4 based on how well the answer meets the criteria listed.
- It should describe how volcanoes are powerful events and describe the harm they can do.
- It may refer to the damage done to Pompeii and to details given about the force, power, or effect of volcanoes.
- It should use relevant details from both passages.
- It should be well-organized, clear, and easy to understand.

Set 8: Literary Texts

Sarah's Diary

Core Skills Practice

Core skill: Refer to details and examples in a text

Answer: The student should explain how writing in the diary relaxes Sarah. The answer should refer to how she feels better after writing in her diary or no longer feels angry or upset after she writes in her diary.

Question	Answer	Common Core Reading Standard
1	A	Determine the meaning of words and phrases as they are used in a text, including those that allude to significant characters found in mythology.
2	D	Describe in depth a character, setting, or event in a story or drama, drawing on specific details in the text.
3	C	Refer to details and examples in a text when explaining what the text says explicitly and when drawing inferences from the text.
4	C	Determine the meaning of words and phrases as they are used in a text, including those that allude to significant characters found in mythology.

Penny the Princess

Core Skills Practice

Core skill: Understand cause and effect / Summarize a text

Answer: The student should explain that meeting the homeless man makes Penny realize how lucky she is or makes her decide to use her powers to help people.

Question	Answer	Common Core Reading Standard
1	D	Determine the meaning of words and phrases as they are used in a text, including those that allude to significant characters found in mythology.
2	A	Determine a theme of a story, drama, or poem from details in the text; summarize the text.
3	D	Explain major differences between poems, drama, and prose, and refer to the structural elements of poems and drama when writing or speaking about a text.
4	1st and 3rd	Explain major differences between poems, drama, and prose, and refer to the structural elements of poems and drama when writing or speaking about a text.

The Eagle

Core Skills Practice

Core skill: Refer to details in a text when drawing inferences from the text

Answer: The student should identify that the eagle is watching the water, and should infer that the eagle is looking for fish or food. The answer should explain that the eagle dives down to get food.

Question	Answer	Common Core Reading Standard
1	2	Explain major differences between poems, drama, and prose, and refer to the structural elements of poems and drama when writing or speaking about a text.
2	B	Determine the meaning of words and phrases as they are used in a text, including those that allude to significant characters found in mythology.
3	D	Determine the meaning of words and phrases as they are used in a text, including those that allude to significant characters found in mythology.
4	C	Make connections between the text of a story or drama and a visual or oral presentation of the text, identifying where each version reflects specific descriptions and directions in the text.

Crying Wolf

Core Skills Practice

Core skill: Form and express an opinion based on a text

Answer: The student should give a reasonable explanation of why Jack's plan is selfish. The answer may refer to how he worries his parents, makes his mother return from work to check on him, or takes advantage of his parents being busy in the morning.

Question	Answer	Common Core Reading Standard
1	B	Refer to details and examples in a text when explaining what the text says explicitly and when drawing inferences from the text.
2	C	Describe in depth a character, setting, or event in a story or drama, drawing on specific details in the text.
3	C	Determine a theme of a story, drama, or poem from details in the text; summarize the text.
4	A	Determine the meaning of words and phrases as they are used in a text, including those that allude to significant characters found in mythology.
5	See Below	Determine a theme of a story, drama, or poem from details in the text; summarize the text.

Give a score of 0, 1, 2, 3, or 4 based on how well the answer meets the criteria listed.
- It should identify the main message of the passage as being about always telling the truth, the consequences of lying, or being trusted by others.
- It should use relevant details from the passage.
- It should be well-organized, clear, and easy to understand.

Set 9: Informational Texts

Soccer

Core Skills Practice

Core skill: Form and express an opinion based on a text

Answer: The student should give an opinion on whether the low scores of soccer games would make it exciting. The answer could agree with the author that waiting for a goal for so long would make it exciting, or could argue that the lack of goals would make the game boring.

Question	Answer	Common Core Reading Standard
1	A	Determine the meaning of general academic and domain-specific words or phrases in a text relevant to a grade 4 topic or subject area.
2	D	Compare and contrast a firsthand and secondhand account of the same event or topic; describe the differences in focus and the information provided.
3	England 1800s	Refer to details and examples in a text when explaining what the text says explicitly and when drawing inferences from the text.
4	A	Interpret information presented visually, orally, or quantitatively and explain how the information contributes to an understanding of the text in which it appears.

Alexander Graham Bell

Core Skills Practice

Core skill: Refer to details in a text when drawing inferences from the text

Answer: The student should make a valid inference about how Elisha Gray would have felt. The inference could be that Gray felt annoyed, angry, disappointed, or jealous.

Question	Answer	Common Core Reading Standard
1	D	Determine the main idea of a text and explain how it is supported by key details; summarize the text.
2	A	Compare and contrast a firsthand and secondhand account of the same event or topic; describe the differences in focus and the information provided.
3	C	Explain how an author uses reasons and evidence to support particular points in a text.
4	C	Refer to details and examples in a text when explaining what the text says explicitly and when drawing inferences from the text.

The First World War

Core Skills Practice

Core skill: Explain ideas in a historical text

Answer: The student should complete the table by listing the Central Powers as Austria, Hungary, and Germany, and the Allies as England, France, Russia, and the United States.

Question	Answer	Common Core Reading Standard
1	B	Interpret information presented visually, orally, or quantitatively and explain how the information contributes to an understanding of the text in which it appears.
2	A	Compare and contrast a firsthand and secondhand account of the same event or topic; describe the differences in focus and the information provided.
3	D	Determine the main idea of a text and explain how it is supported by key details; summarize the text.
4	C	Determine the meaning of general academic and domain-specific words or phrases in a text relevant to a grade 4 topic or subject area.

Camels

Core Skills Practice

Core skill: Describe the structure of information in a text

Answer: The student should identify the topic of the second paragraph as being about how camels go without water, and the topic of the third paragraph as being about where camels live.

Question	Answer	Common Core Reading Standard
1	C	Explain events, procedures, ideas, or concepts in a historical, scientific, or technical text, including what happened and why, based on specific information in the text.
2	C	Compare and contrast a firsthand and secondhand account of the same event or topic.
3	B	Determine the main idea of a text and explain how it is supported by key details; summarize the text.
4	A	Determine the meaning of general academic and domain-specific words or phrases in a text relevant to a grade 4 topic or subject area.
5	See Below	Explain events, procedures, ideas, or concepts in a historical, scientific, or technical text, including what happened and why, based on specific information in the text.

Give a score of 0, 1, 2, 3, or 4 based on how well the answer meets the criteria listed.
- It should provide an explanation of how a camel's hump helps it survive.
- The answer should include that the hump stores fat, and that the fat is used for energy.
- It should use relevant details from the passage.
- It should be well-organized, clear, and easy to understand.

Set 10: Informational Texts

Book Review

Core Skills Practice

Core skill: Explain how authors use reasons to support particular points

Answer: The student should describe how the second paragraph supports the idea that Jack learned to express his thoughts. The student should refer to Jack writing about the day his dog got hit by a car.

Question	Answer	Common Core Reading Standard
1	A	Refer to details and examples in a text when explaining what the text says explicitly and when drawing inferences from the text.
2	C	Describe the overall structure (e.g., chronology, comparison, cause/effect, problem/solution) of events, ideas, concepts, or information in a text or part of a text.
3	D	Compare and contrast a firsthand and secondhand account of the same event or topic; describe the differences in focus and the information provided.
4	D	Determine the meaning of general academic and domain-specific words or phrases in a text relevant to a grade 4 topic or subject area.

Beekeeping

Core Skills Practice

Core skill: Interpret information presented visually

Answer: The student should relate the photograph to passage content. The student should identify that the beekeeper is wearing protective gear and relate this to how beekeepers used to have to wear suits to protect them from bees.

Question	Answer	Common Core Reading Standard
1	A	Refer to details and examples in a text when explaining what the text says explicitly and when drawing inferences from the text.
2	C	Explain events, procedures, ideas, or concepts in a historical, scientific, or technical text, including what happened and why, based on specific information in the text.
3	C	Determine the main idea of a text and explain how it is supported by key details; summarize the text.
4	D	Interpret information presented visually, orally, or quantitatively and explain how the information contributes to an understanding of the text in which it appears.

Pizza Party Flyer

Core Skills Practice
Core skill: Integrate information from two texts on the same topic
Answer: The student should describe details that suggest that the atmosphere will be fun. The answer may refer to phrases like "eat your heart out" and "have fun with your friends." The answer may also refer to the free pizza and the entertainment and activities.

Question	Answer	Common Core Reading Standard
1	A	Compare and contrast a firsthand and secondhand account of the same event or topic; describe the differences in focus and the information provided.
2	Feb 14 Saturday 2 to 6 p.m. Dom's Italian	Refer to details and examples in a text when explaining what the text says explicitly and when drawing inferences from the text.
3	C	Integrate information from two texts on the same topic in order to write or speak about the subject knowledgeably.
4	C	Determine the main idea of a text and explain how it is supported by key details; summarize the text.

Yoga

Core Skills Practice
Core skill: Integrate information from two texts on the same topic
Answer: The student should describe three features that show that the passage and poster is aimed at beginners. The answer could describe how the passage refers to starting with simple poses and refers to getting started. The answer could describe how the poster refers to giving yoga a go, mentions not needing anything special to start, and refers to five poses that everyone can do.

Question	Answer	Common Core Reading Standard
1	Downward-Facing Dog Child's Pose	Refer to details and examples in a text when explaining what the text says explicitly and when drawing inferences from the text.
2	B	Compare and contrast a firsthand and secondhand account of the same event or topic; describe the differences in focus and the information provided.
3	D	Explain how an author uses reasons and evidence to support particular points in a text.
4	B	Integrate information from two texts on the same topic in order to write or speak about the subject knowledgeably.
5	See Below	Write opinion pieces on topics or texts, supporting a point of view with reasons and information.

Give a score of 0, 1, 2, 3, or 4 based on how well the answer meets the criteria listed.
- It should persuade students to try yoga.
- The answer should include reasons that students should try yoga.
- It should use relevant details from the passage.
- It should be well-organized, clear, and easy to understand.

Set 11: Literary and Informational Texts

Herbal Tea

Core Skills Practice

Core skill: Interpret information and describe how it contributes to understanding

Answer: The student should describe two ways the information in the sidebar would influence a reader. The answer could refer to how people would want to drink herbal tea or to how people would choose what type of tea to drink.

Question	Answer	Common Core Reading Standard
1	B	Determine the meaning of general academic and domain-specific words or phrases in a text relevant to a grade 4 topic or subject area.
2	A	Determine the main idea of a text and explain how it is supported by key details; summarize the text.
3	2, 4, 3, 1	Explain events, procedures, ideas, or concepts in a historical, scientific, or technical text, including what happened and why, based on specific information in the text.
4	Steps 3, 4, and 6	Refer to details and examples in a text when explaining what the text says explicitly and when drawing inferences from the text.

Fish Food

Core Skills Practice

Core skill: Describe a setting, drawing on specific details in the text

Answer: The student should give reasonable answers to the questions. Sample answers are given below.
Where does this story take place? at a lake
What time of day do you think the story takes place? around noon
What time of year do you think the story takes place? summer

Question	Answer	Common Core Reading Standard
1	B	Refer to details and examples in a text when explaining what the text says explicitly and when drawing inferences from the text.
2	B	Refer to details and examples in a text when explaining what the text says explicitly and when drawing inferences from the text.
3	A	Determine a theme of a story, drama, or poem from details in the text; summarize the text.
4	B	Describe in depth a character, setting, or event in a story or drama, drawing on specific details in the text.

The Capybara

Core Skills Practice

Core skill: Compare two items / Make inferences based on information in a text

Answer: The student should identify that capybaras have more in common with beavers. The supporting details may include information from the passage such as the size of capybaras and how capybaras live near water, or information gathered from the photograph.

Question	Answer	Common Core Reading Standard
1	See Below	Refer to details and examples in a text when explaining what the text says explicitly and when drawing inferences from the text.
2	C	Determine the meaning of general academic and domain-specific words or phrases in a text relevant to a grade 4 topic or subject area.
3	C	Compare and contrast a firsthand and secondhand account of the same event or topic; describe the differences in focus and the information provided.
4	B	Describe the overall structure (e.g., chronology, comparison, cause/effect, problem/solution) of events, ideas, concepts, or information in a text or part of a text.

The student should list the following: beavers, squirrels, chipmunks, rats, mice, capybaras.

The Light

Core Skills Practice

Core skill: Describe an event in a story, drawing on specific details in the text

Answer: The student should explain how the author helps the reader imagine the light. The answer may refer to how the light seemed to shimmer, seemed to dance, or changed colors.

Question	Answer	Common Core Reading Standard
1	C	Determine the meaning of words and phrases as they are used in a text, including those that allude to significant characters found in mythology.
2	C	Compare and contrast the point of view from which different stories are narrated, including the difference between first- and third-person narrations.
3	D	Describe in depth a character, setting, or event in a story or drama, drawing on specific details in the text.
4	B	Determine a theme of a story, drama, or poem from details in the text; summarize the text.
5	See Below	Refer to details and examples in a text when explaining what the text says explicitly and when drawing inferences from the text.

Give a score of 0, 1, 2, 3, or 4 based on how well the answer meets the criteria listed.
- It should make a reasonable prediction about what happens next in the passage.
- The prediction made should be at least partly based on details given in the passage.
- It should be well-organized, clear, and easy to understand.

Set 12: Literary and Informational Texts

Thank You

Core Skills Practice

Core skill: Make connections between text and a visual presentation of the text

Answer: The student should identify that the photograph shows that Lucy received many presents for her birthday.

Question	Answer	Common Core Reading Standard
1	D	Determine the meaning of words and phrases as they are used in a text, including those that allude to significant characters found in mythology.
2	C	Determine the meaning of words and phrases as they are used in a text, including those that allude to significant characters found in mythology.
3	A	Describe in depth a character, setting, or event in a story or drama, drawing on specific details in the text.
4	A	Refer to details and examples in a text when explaining what the text says explicitly and when drawing inferences from the text.

A Day in the Life

Core Skills Practice

Core skill: Refer to details in a text when explaining what a text says

Answer: The student should identify details that show that Jenny is proud of her father. The answer may refer to how she asks about his day, is amazed by him, thinks he is ready for anything, or wants to be like him.

Question	Answer	Common Core Reading Standard
1	D	Determine the meaning of words and phrases as they are used in a text, including those that allude to significant characters found in mythology.
2	A	Determine a theme of a story, drama, or poem from details in the text; summarize the text.
3	See Below	Refer to details and examples in a text when explaining what the text says explicitly and when drawing inferences from the text.
4	D	Explain major differences between poems, drama, and prose, and refer to the structural elements of poems and drama when writing or speaking about a text.

The student should list the following: tracks down thieves, directs traffic.

Silver

Core Skills Practice

Core skill: Interpret information presented quantitatively (in charts and graphs)

Answer: The student should explain that the graph shows the different uses of silver and shows how much silver is used for each purpose.

Question	Answer	Common Core Reading Standard
1	C	Determine the meaning of general academic and domain-specific words or phrases in a text relevant to a grade 4 topic or subject area.
2	D	Explain events, procedures, ideas, or concepts in a historical, scientific, or technical text, including what happened and why, based on specific information in the text.
3	C	Determine the main idea of a text and explain how it is supported by key details; summarize the text.
4	A	Determine the meaning of general academic and domain-specific words or phrases in a text relevant to a grade 4 topic or subject area.

Creature Comforts

Core Skills Practice

Core skill: Refer to details in a text when drawing inferences from the text

Answer: The student should explain that Fred is happy and content. The student should refer to how Fred just wants his animals to be happy.

Question	Answer	Common Core Reading Standard
1	C	Determine the meaning of words and phrases as they are used in a text, including those that allude to significant characters found in mythology.
2	A	Explain major differences between poems, drama, and prose, and refer to the structural elements of poems and drama when writing or speaking about a text.
3	A	Describe in depth a character, setting, or event in a story or drama, drawing on specific details in the text.
4	D	Refer to details and examples in a text when explaining what the text says explicitly and when drawing inferences from the text.
5	See Below	Describe in depth a character, setting, or event in a story or drama, drawing on specific details in the text.

Give a score of 0, 1, 2, 3, or 4 based on how well the answer meets the criteria listed.
- It should give details from the passage that show that life on the farm is hard.
- It may refer to the weather, to the long days, or to how there is always something to be done.
- It should use relevant details from the passage.
- It should be well-organized, clear, and easy to understand.

Set 13: Paired Literary Texts

Soccer/Something Special

Core Skills Practice
Core skill: Determine a theme of a story
Answer: The student should give a title that relates to the message of the passage, such as "A Surprising Choice" or "Girls Can Play Too!" The student should explain why the title suits the passage.

Core Skills Practice
Core skill: Understand and compare point of view
Answer: The student should write a paragraph describing Toby being dropped from the team. The narrative should be written in first-person point of view.

Question	Answer	Common Core Reading Standard
1	C	Determine the meaning of words and phrases as they are used in a text, including those that allude to significant characters found in mythology.
2	A	Refer to details and examples in a text when explaining what the text says explicitly and when drawing inferences from the text.
3	B	Describe in depth a character, setting, or event in a story or drama, drawing on specific details in the text.
4	B	Explain major differences between poems, drama, and prose, and refer to the structural elements of poems and drama when writing or speaking about a text.
5	See Below	Determine a theme of a story, drama, or poem from details in the text; summarize the text.
6	A	Refer to details and examples in a text when explaining what the text says explicitly and when drawing inferences from the text.
7	A	Explain major differences between poems, drama, and prose, and refer to the structural elements of poems and drama when writing or speaking about a text.
8	A	Determine a theme of a story, drama, or poem from details in the text; summarize the text.
9	B	Determine the meaning of words and phrases as they are used in a text, including those that allude to significant characters found in mythology.
10	See Below	Compare and contrast the treatment of similar themes and topics and patterns of events in stories, myths, and traditional literature from different cultures.
11	See Below	Compare and contrast the treatment of similar themes and topics and patterns of events in stories, myths, and traditional literature from different cultures.
12	See Below	Compare and contrast the treatment of similar themes and topics and patterns of events in stories, myths, and traditional literature from different cultures.

Q5.
Give a score of 0, 1, 2, 3, or 4 based on how well the answer meets the criteria listed.
- It should explain how the brothers support Molly.
- It may describe how they let her play soccer with them, how they teach her new skills, or how they are happy when she is chosen for the team.
- It should use relevant details from the passage.
- It should be well-organized, clear, and easy to understand.

Q10.
Give a score of 0, 1, or 2 based on how well the answer meets the criteria listed.
- It should explain that Molly and Toby both love playing their sport or that their sport means a lot to them both. It may identify other similarities, such as how they both are happy with any chance to play, both want to be part of a team, or both like practicing and getting better.

Q11.
Give a score of 0, 1, or 2 based on how well the answer meets the criteria listed.
- It should identify that Molly and Toby develop strong skills by playing as much as they can and by practicing on their own.
- The answer may identify either of these as the similarity between how they develop their skills.

Q12.
Give a score of 0, 1, 2, 3, or 4 based on how well the answer meets the criteria listed.
- It should give a reasonable description of how Molly and Toby feel when they are picked.
- Molly could be described as excited, surprised, or pleased. Toby could be described as relieved or happy.
- It should include an explanation of why they each feel that way.
- It should use relevant details from both passages.
- It should be well-organized, clear, and easy to understand.

Set 14: Paired Informational Texts

Brain Size/Ants Seeking Food

Core Skills Practice
Core skill: Compare and contrast two items / Explain concepts in a scientific text
Answer: The student should list how the brain of an ant is smaller, makes up a larger portion of its body weight, and has less ability.

Core Skills Practice
Core skill: Describe the structure of information in a text
Answer: The student should explain why the author begins by asking how people find food. The student may describe how it creates interest, makes the reader curious, or helps the reader relate to the ants.

Question	Answer	Common Core Reading Standard
1	A	Compare and contrast a firsthand and secondhand account of the same event or topic; describe the differences in focus and the information provided.
2	A	Describe the overall structure (e.g., chronology, comparison, cause/effect, problem/solution) of events, ideas, concepts, or information in a text or part of a text.
3	D	Refer to details and examples in a text when explaining what the text says explicitly and when drawing inferences from the text.
4	C	Interpret information presented visually, orally, or quantitatively and explain how the information contributes to an understanding of the text in which it appears.
5	B	Determine the meaning of general academic and domain-specific words or phrases in a text relevant to a grade 4 topic or subject area.
6	C	Explain how an author uses reasons and evidence to support particular points in a text.
7	D	Describe the overall structure (e.g., chronology, comparison, cause/effect, problem/solution) of events, ideas, concepts, or information in a text or part of a text.
8	A	Determine the main idea of a text and explain how it is supported by key details; summarize the text.
9	See Below	Integrate information from two texts on the same topic in order to write or speak about the subject knowledgeably.

Q9.
Give a score of 0, 1, 2, 3, or 4 based on how well the answer meets the criteria listed.
- It should explain how ants work together and why ants work together.
- It should refer to specific information given about ants having different roles, ants living in large groups, or ants helping each other find food.
- It should use relevant details from both passages.
- It should be well-organized, clear, and easy to understand.

Get to Know Our Product Range

Mathematics

Practice Test Books
Practice sets and practice tests will prepare students for the state tests.

Common Core Quiz Books
Focused individual quizzes cover every math skill one by one.

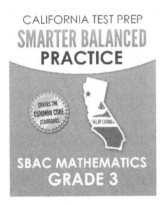 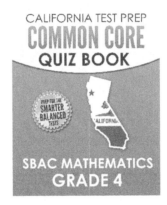 

English Language Arts/Reading

Practice Test Books
Practice sets and practice tests will prepare students for the state tests.

Reading Skills Workbooks
Short passages and question sets will develop and improve reading comprehension skills and are perfect for ongoing test prep.

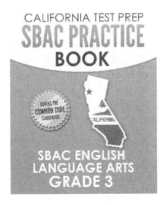 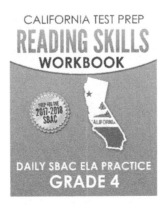 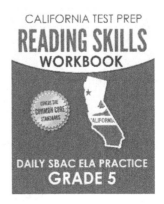

Writing

Writing Skills Workbooks
Students write narratives, essays, and opinion pieces, and write in response to passages.

Persuasive and Narrative Writing Workbooks
Guided workbooks teach all the skills needed to write narratives and opinion pieces.

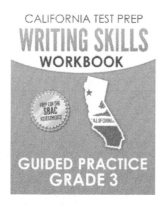 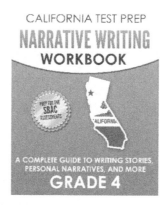 

Language and Vocabulary

Language and Vocabulary Quiz Books
Focused quizzes cover spelling, grammar, usage, writing conventions, and vocabulary.

Revising and Editing Workbooks
Students improve language skills and writing skills by identifying and correcting errors.

Language Skills Workbooks
Exercises on specific language skills including figurative language, synonyms, and homographs.

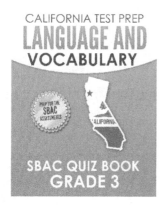 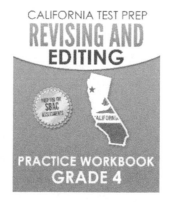 

http://www.testmasterpress.com

Made in the USA
Las Vegas, NV
19 December 2024